EDUCATION
for
WHAT IS REAL

EDUCATION
for
WHAT IS REAL

❖❖❖❖❖❖❖❖❖❖❖❖❖❖❖❖❖❖❖❖❖❖❖❖❖❖❖❖❖❖❖❖❖❖

EARL C. KELLEY

Professor of Secondary Education
Wayne University, Detroit, Michigan

FOREWORD BY JOHN DEWEY

HARPER & BROTHERS PUBLISHERS
❖❖❖❖❖❖❖❖❖❖❖❖❖❖❖❖❖❖❖❖❖❖❖❖❖❖❖❖❖❖❖❖❖❖

New York and London

To
Adelbert Ames, Jr.
and
John Pearson

LC 47-12211

EDUCATION FOR WHAT IS REAL

Copyright, 1947, by Earl C. Kelley
Printed in the United States of America

C-F

Foreword

By John Dewey

In the following pages Professor Kelley has restated at the outset some educational principles and standards that have been urged upon teachers more or less often in the last half century. If he had not gone beyond that, his book would have been welcome in its vigor and clarity. But it goes definitely beyond that. I doubt if many persons who have been active in forwarding the newer movements in public education during the years mentioned would say today that they were satisfied with what has been accomplished in spite of bright points on the horizon. There are many reasons for this situation. But one is particularly pertinent to the present book.

Excellent reasons have been offered for adoption of the principles which underlie the new processes and conditions of the public school. But none of them had the force of out-and-out demonstration. They did not even have the outward parade of the external mechanics put out by some theories but which nevertheless were lacking in grasp of what is so distinctively human in life that no amount of such parade could begin to make up for its absence. In fact, in many cases it was used simply to add to the efficiency of older mechanical life-chilling and hardening operations.

This phase of the situation is now radically changed. Under the inspiration and direction of Dr. Adelbert Ames of the Hanover Institute, there has been developed an ex-

1814

perimental demonstration of the principles which govern the development of perceiving, principles which are found, moreover, to operate more deeply in the basic growth of human beings in their distinctively human capacity than any which have been previously laid bare.

I am aware that these are strong words. As Professor Kelley remarks in his book, "It is not the first writing that has been done on this topic, nor, I predict, will it be the last." The inherent convincingness of the work of Dr. Ames and his associates goes, however, too deep to be welcome in some influential quarters. It will probably take a good many years for it to go through that succession of stages until it will be said, "Oh, that theory; why, everybody always knew that was true." I am, accordingly, especially grateful to Dr. Kelley for permitting me to have a part in calling attention to a work whose significance will prove virtually inexhaustible.

Contents

Preface

This book is a report on the significance to education of the findings in the nature of perception, of knowing, and of life itself, by the searchers after truth who have worked in the laboratories of The Hanover Institute (formerly Dartmouth Eye Institute). It is not the first writing that has been done on this topic, nor, I predict, will it be the last. But it is what a teacher saw there, together with the implications which can be drawn by a teacher.

For a long time I have felt that there is more involved in knowing, than many of us teachers had assumed or understood. The idea of teaching by precept, for example, has long seemed too simple to account for what goes on in the learning process. There are too many unanswered questions. Why is a fine painting better than a photograph? In the usual concept of seeing the photograph ought to be better than the painting, because it is more accurate and detailed. But it fails to satisfy as the painting does. What do we really mean by "satisfy"? Is there a relationship or a communion between man and his environment? Where do I leave off and my environment begin? And in saying "I," do I refer to my brain, heart, eye, or toe?

A considerable amount has been written lately about the wholeness of man; in part it is meant by this that man is one with his environment, that the connection between man and his externality is more close than has been so long assumed. Man seems to be more than just a receiving station for light rays reflected by the objects around him. Perhaps he makes his surroundings what they really are. And this is what is meant by the oneness of man and his environment.

Certain it is that the basis of knowing is perception, and a real understanding of perception, going beyond the naïve receiving station concept, will enable us to understand more clearly the nature of man himself. It is in the act or the miracle of perception that contact is established with externality, that experience and growth become possible, and that meaning comes into being.

Granting that some of the above is hindsight, the problem bothered me enough so that when I received an invitation to spend two days at the laboratories of The Hanover Institute, I accepted at some inconvenience to myself. After the two days were over, I was bothered much more than ever. I think I was enlightened hardly at all, but I had ten questions to ask myself where before I had had one. So in the summer of 1946 I spent ten weeks in Hanover, New Hampshire, tried to push my thinking further, and to make some sort of record of what I learned. The record, much revised, follows in this book.

To say that the studies are important is, in my opinion, to betray the weakness of words. I believe that these experiments go far to supply, in a material, laboratory way, what has been lacking in our understanding of the relation between the human organism and his environment, and all that this implies—for education, art, diplomacy, human relations, and so on. Speaking as a teacher, I believe that if we really master these basic facts of perception, they will tell us how to arrange for the growth of children, and from this point of departure we can finally establish what we may believe about teaching and learning.

As for the book, it is a faltering first step, tentative and incomplete. It is written, I hope, so that most readers can understand it. Many ideas are left out because I lacked the skill to explain them in simple terms. I argue beyond the experiments, it is true, but I use the experiments for a base and try not to violate any of the principles laid down by them. I see different implications from those that would have been seen by any other observer, and that is in keeping with the experiments.

Some of my friends who have read the manuscript feel that Chapter I is not necessary to the book, and not related to it. But it seems necessary to me that I should establish the fact that all is not well with the world. If this is not true, if all is well, then a new approach to man's problems is not needed.

Others have been bothered by the lack of references and documentation. But I can hardly depend for proof on the mere fact that someone else said it before. We have a strange faith in what has been put into print. Once the type is set, the statement becomes authority. Just to show that I did not make everything up out of my own head, I did footnote a statement in Chapter I on what we spend for education. But where did the fellow I quoted get his information? Or is the fact that I can point to the printed word enough?

When it comes to acknowledgments, I must first mention Professor Adelbert Ames, Jr., of The Hanover Institute. It was only by personally experiencing the numerous visual phenomena made patent by his demonstrations that I could grasp and understand the nature of perception. In one sense, therefore, he should have been a co-author. But he insists he has no background of experience in the field of education and that the essence of what I have presented is my knowledge and experience in that field as affected by my enlarged understanding of the nature of perception. The basic hypothesis elaborated throughout the book is that one cannot learn by authority but only by experience. It follows that the building up of his name or mine, which might cause those interested to look for the final answer in authority rather than in their own concrete experiences, would defeat the purposes of the presentation.

We agreed on two restrictions on my writing. One, that I write so that "Joe Doakes" could understand, and that any idea that could not be explained in ordinary English probably wouldn't make much difference anyway, for he sees that it is the understanding in the hearts and minds of the common people that may make a difference. The other restriction was that I keep it short. If some of the ideas in the book seem a bit underdone, please remember that I had instructions to make it short and plain.

Mr. John Pearson, administrative head of the Institute, in another way, has been almost as responsible for the development of the research as has Professor Ames. He is a businessman who sees the deep significance of the development and who has moved mountains to keep it going, with great sacrifice to himself. He has been evangelistic in his zeal, and has kept the project alive.

Dr. Marie I. Rasey, Professor of Educational Psychology at Wayne University, poet and scientist, has made two trips to Hanover so as to be able to check ideas with me. Her broad knowledge of science, especially psychology, has been invaluable. While we perforce did not see precisely the same things in the laboratories, we were able to combine our observations into a statment in which I could have confidence.

Special thanks are due Dr. and Mrs. William H. Kilpatrick for their assistance. They both read the original manuscript and made special notes for my guidance. They made a trip to Hanover to see if they could see what I saw. They have both given of their time since, in letters, committee meetings, and in helping to push my ideas a little further than they could have gone otherwise.

Dr. Howard A. Lane, of New York University, also made a trip to Hanover and then carefully checked over the manuscript. Dr. John C. Sullivan, Educational Psychologist at Wayne University, went over the whole manuscript with me with great care, to check ideas and the manner of expressing them.

Others who have read the first draft and given me the benefit of their comments in writing, both confirmatory and critical, are Dr. Charles M. MacConnell, Director of The New School, Evanston Township High School, Evanston, Illinois; Gregory Bateson, Institute of Intercultural Studies, New York; Dr. Kenneth Benne, Teachers College, Columbia University; Professor Ross Mooney and Professor Hoyt Sherman of Ohio State University; Professor William H. Burton of Harvard University; Dean Waldo E. Lessenger, College of Education, Wayne University; Dr. Jane B. Welling and Miss Jessie Wedin of Wayne University; Dr. Whit Brogan, Bureau of Intercultural Education, New York; Laurentine B. Collins, Director of School and Community Relations, Detroit Public Schools; and Donald Slutz, Director, Traffic Safety Association, Detroit. My wife and daughter have read and criticized as I wrote. My daughter, who is fifteen, has served as my anchor to the people. Ideas which she did not understand were revised or taken out. That is one way in which I endeavored to keep in touch with Professor Ames' Joe Doakes.

Detroit, Michigan   THE AUTHOR
April 15, 1947

CHAPTER I

How Can These Things Be?

The following comments are not cheerful. Would that the current scene could be honestly viewed and happily described. But, unhappily, we have learned how to destroy each other before we have learned to like each other. And unless we can learn to like each other before our mutual feelings of distrust result in action, we are lost. This is a large order, but not a hopeless one. We *can* start to lay down patterns of living which will enable us to survive. It is my hope that a look at our present scene will help us to face our necessities; and thus this is not a counsel of despair. Let us look at ourselves first, and plan our action in the light of, and in the face of, what we see.

It was not long ago that we received the glad news that our last enemy had surrendered, and that the big guns could at last stop firing on a bloodsoaked world. No more would our own kind need to die in far-off places; they could now come home and live in peace among the scenes so dear to them. We declared a two-day holiday, we danced in the streets, and each one of us celebrated according to his own manner of expressing joy. Now we were to enter into the glories of that postwar world of which we had dreamed so long and for which we had sacrificed so much.

We had come to the end of another of those adven-

tures in bloodshed during which we periodically fall
upon each other bent on utter destruction. We told ourselves that, although the record had been bad, this
surely was the end of wars and that a permanent and
universal peace was about to be achieved. For the twen-
tieth century, though less than half done, had already
established itself as the bloodiest in human history.[1] In
fact, more people had died by violence in the first half
of this century than in all of recorded history combined.
It had seemed that man was bent upon his own complete destruction by the violence of his own hand.

It was not long, however, before we could see that the
war did not end with the signing of the papers in Tokyo
Bay. For four years we had been fighting foreign villains,
men strange to us who threatened our "way of life."
During this time we seemed to achieve a commonalty of
purpose, and it seemed that we had achieved a sort of
brotherhood through this common purpose. When the
common foe was vanquished, we lost our common purpose and began again to fight among ourselves. Our problems became much more complex, because our enemy
was not a peculiar stranger, but our own kind. Our
enemy did not live in a foreign land, but he was among
us, walking our own streets, sharing our polling places,
working at the machine next to ours.

What kind of madness was this? How could it come
about? It is difficult to describe the battles and campaigns
of a diffused warfare, because no one event happens
clearly before another, but some of the many battle
fronts can be set forth, though probably not in their
proper order.

[1] For a really devastating summary of man's achievement in bloodshed during the first half of this enlightened century, see the first
chapter of "Education and World Tragedy," by Howard Mumford
Jones (Harvard Press, 1946).

First we fell out with our brothers-in-arms. In the bitter campaign of the summer of 1942, when the enemy was surging to the gates of Stalingrad; when he stood before Alexandria; when his U-boats were sinking our American ships within sight of our own shores; then we called the Russian brother. We poured supplies to him, and as he stood up to the most deadly war machines in history, his valor and virtue were legendary. But instantly upon the collapse of our cause for brotherhood, both sides withdrew from each other and began to regard each other with suspicion.

Within a matter of weeks, one could hear the statement that the world is not big enough for both the Russians and us, and the quicker we went to war with them and "had it out," the better. A few months before it was Nazi Germany who could not live with us. Maybe nobody can. We thanked God for the atomic bomb, which *we* had and *they* hadn't. We speeded the manufacture of them, and held them in strategic places. We talked peace and understanding to our erstwhile friends while holding a gun in their ribs.

The Russians, of course, acted no better. Maybe it is difficult to act natural under poised atomic bombs. Fear, suspicion, and greed seemed to be their motivating forces in international affairs. We had been their blood brothers in their dire need of 1942. Now we became capitalist imperialists. The ghost of Hitler must have laughed!

We brothers-in-arms began to quarrel about who should have what territory. In Java, American lend-lease guns cut down the inhabitants who wanted nothing but the right to live their own lives in the land of their birth. The citizens of French Indo-China found themselves still fighting Japanese troops, but now employed by the French. The fate of India and Africa was much discussed, without any consideration for the wishes or welfare of the people living there.

At home, we began to turn our bloodthirsty attention to our own minorities. During the war we had been lacking in man power, so many of our depressed peoples had been brought into use and had attained an economic status never before enjoyed by them. We were confronted with the problem of putting them back in their proper places. They were holding jobs we wanted. When we needed man power, we had passed a law providing fair employment practices to all peoples regardless of color or creed. Now that the need had passed, our Congress debated the renewal of the law, long and loud, with filibusters and all that goes with a good congressional brawl, and finally decided in favor of unfair employment practices.

One of the great rallying cries of the war was the Nazi attitude and action toward minorities, and the theory of the master race. Now we must hastily regain the race mastery we almost lost while we were smashing Hitler's race mastery. That hardy perennial of bigotry and hatred, the Ku Klux Klan, has again crawled out of the mire, declaring that some Americans may live, others must die, either by violence or starvation.

But our venom has not been confined to peoples who happen to have been born with different colored skins or different racial backgrounds. Our hands have been raised against our own blood brothers.

The present struggle between capital and labor, with each taking counsel from fear and appealing to force of one kind or another, is typical. There are many others. National propaganda organizations are hard at work in an effort to drive us apart. Each is seeking his own advantage no matter what the cost to the rest. Each usually justifies his selfish act with the pious statement that if he has his way, those whom he hopes to take advantage of will be somehow better off.

During the war, probably more lip service was paid to our love of the men and women in the field than to any other group. They were of us, our own flesh and blood, slugging it out with our cruel and efficient enemy. They had not had too good going during the thirties. They were largely the "lost generation," for whom there had been no place in our society when they attained adulthood. Now they were out there, throwing their bodies before the oncoming war machine of our enemies. Many of them were giving their lives that we might live in the bright new postwar world. We longed for the day of their return, and nothing would ever be too good for them.

Now they are returned veterans; and believe it or not, we are at war with them too. One can hear angry debate as to their seniority rights on their old jobs. Many of them are married, have babies, and want places to live. It is perfectly possible for us to house every one of our returned veterans decently. It is not nearly the task that building our fleet was. But because of one pressure group or another, materials cannot be found for this purpose, and the men and women who fought for their homes are living with relatives, or existing in substandard rooms. Many of their marriages are going to pieces because of impossible living conditions. But we care more for an advantage here or there than we do for the comfort and happiness of those who fought for us.

Many veterans want a college education, but our educational plant is so small and inadequate that there is no room for them. Those who have succeeded in getting into college have found conditions so crowded and the procedure so much like an assembly line that they are not

profiting as much as they should. We have known for
five years that when the war ended our facilities for higher
education would not do the job, but we have done virtually nothing to meet the situation. When we know a
condition in advance, and do nothing about it, one is
forced to the conclusion that we do not really care about
it, or have some undisclosed reason for failing to take
action. We do have a few Quonset huts on our campuses
to offer. The chances are that the veteran can pass his
evening hours in a new nearby roadhouse, built of materials which would make fine homes or dormitories.

Closely related to the plight of the veteran, though not
limited to the postwar era, is our characteristic neglect of
our young people. They are our most valuable asset, but
we really do not care greatly about them, if it is fair to
judge by what we do. During the depression, we hugged
our dwindling securities to our bosoms, while the carriers
of the hope of the human race wasted its powers in use-
lessness. But in normal times we do not do much better,
except, of course, in wartime when we need manpower.
We give our children, especially in large cities, such miser-
able conditions under which to grow up that many of
them become delinquent. Delinquency is a measure of
adult neglect of children, for the children are all right
when we get them. Their undesirable characteristics are
all learned in an adult-managed world. When they become too bothersome, we put them in institutions run the
cheapest way possible. We leave them in these crime
schools until they are certain to be completely incapable
of normal useful lives.

We provide so-called education for our children, but
it is miserably supported. The buildings are mostly old
and crowded. The teachers are underpaid, ill-prepared,
and overworked. They have so many children in their

classes that about the best they can give is custodial care. We value our children so little that we spend over twice as much for alcoholic beverages alone as we do for education.

WE ARE MOTIVATED BY FEAR

The outstanding characteristic of our age seems to be fear. Man has of course always known fear, but as our capacity to destroy has grown, our enemies have become less identifiable, and their capacity to strike has increased, so that our apprehension has become less reasoned. When I speak of fear, I wish to differentiate between prudence or caution, and anxiety or emotional fear. Prudence is a reasoned caution, based on observable facts. It is the decision not to take the calculated risk; or if to take it, in what manner. It is choice of time and terrain for reduction of risks which seem necessary. It is part of the problem-solving process, since in the solution of almost any problem, certain greater or less risks are involved. For example, if I choose not to go through an alley at night, but to walk around the block, it is because I know that people are sometimes assaulted in dark alleys and that the advantage would be all with the assailant. The extra time involved in walking around is trifling and I judge the short time saved not to be worth the calculated risk. This is not fear in the sense here used.

Fear is an emotion, not based on reason, not involving calculated risk, and not subject to rational processes. In its milder form, it might better be called anxiety or apprehension. Being emotional rather than rational, it is difficult to overcome by rational processes, and the ends to which it can drive one are as unpredictable as its source is ill-defined.

The most charitable explanation we can make as to why

our hands are everywhere turned against our brothers is that we are terribly and ignominously afraid. We are afraid of the Russians, and they are afraid of us. Those of us with white skins are afraid of the Negroes, and the Negroes are afraid of white people. We are afraid to admit strangers to our shores. Gentiles fear Jews, and make up stories about them to make their fears seem rational. We do not feel safe just fearing people who are different from us. We fear neighbor, fellow church-member, blood relative. So our actions toward each other are colored by one of our most destructive emotions.

Fear is used by parents as a motive from the cradle in controlling their children. Almost the first thing a child understands is a threat. This calls for a corresponding reaction in the child. Children therefore grow up carrying fear and suspicion toward all adults. The church often uses fear to keep its members, and to promote what it considers to be the good life.

Fear is the motivating factor in our schools. Children, for fear of consequences, are made to study what they would not study of their own accord. Even where danger of the indignity of physical punishment has been removed, the fear of failure, the opprobrium of teachers, parents, and worst of all, classmates, hang over our young.

And so it comes about that children learn early to fear and distrust adults—parents and teachers in particular. Teachers fear the children (they might get out of hand) and they fear the school administrator. The administrator fears children, teachers, board of education, and the public in general. Parents so fear the teacher and administrator that they can hardly be dragged to the school for conferences concerning their children, their most valuable asset.

All this adds up to a way of life. It establishes what is

too often our basic approach to other people. We mistrust the motives of the neighbor next door, to say nothing of our attitude toward a strange people far across the sea, whom we have never seen. It is easy to make anyone with such a background hate labor, or employer, or Jew, or Chinese, or Negro, or white.

The step from hatred engendered by fear to violence is a short one and while most of us stop with restrictive measures intended to strangle those we fear, some of us go in for pogroms and lynchings. Some of us even put on bedsheets at night and go around striking terror in the hearts of other people. These strange folks burn fiery crosses to add to this terror, one of a number of odd uses to which the symbol of Christianity is put.

SOME CAN'T TAKE IT

The pattern laid down by compulsion, coercion, and fear, accepted in infancy and projected in age, is a difficult way of life, and for many of us it is completely untenable. When we come to feel that the lives we are leading can no longer operate, we take various means of escape, many of which look fantastic when viewed in the light of what we can imagine as constituting the good life.

One of these is flight into insanity. The human mind simply refuses to accept the situation which it finds abhorrent, and departs into a world of its own—a world more to its liking. The trend toward insanity in this generation is nothing less than appalling. It is said that one out of twenty-two of all of the people in America will at one time during life occupy a bed in a mental hospital.[2]

[2] For more detail on the alarming spread of mental illness see an article by Rudolph G. Novick, "Care And Treatment of the Mentally Ill in Illinois," in DISEASES OF THE NERVOUS SYSTEM, May, 1946, Volume 7, Number 5.

This does not include the millions who need such care but do not get it. There are those who believe that the actions of the Germans and Japanese (particularly the Japanese) in starting World War II represented instances of mass insanity, where a whole people, through damaged feelings of inferiority and through privation, departed from reality. They then started on a program of mass destruction of those who they felt had brought about their condition. If there is truth in this, it is a sobering thought to know that in the world we know, whole masses of people can depart from reality. Perhaps it will engulf us all, or has it?

We are all too familiar with other symptoms of social disorganization to make their repetition particularly useful. It will be sufficient to cite the fact that juvenile delinquency (youth's revolt against an unfriendly world) is steadily on the increase in spite of the fact that we make more effort to curb it than we ever have done before. Often the very methods we use to solve delinquency are in the pattern which caused it. We increase the forces which pursue and apprehend delinquents, and when we no longer know what to do with them, we return them to the environment which caused the delinquency. Almost universally we treat the symptom rather than the cause.

Our society abounds in illustrations of this fact. One does not need to look far for them. In the daily newspaper of the day this is being written,[3] there is an account from Boise, Idaho, describing a scene where a father spanked his seventeen-year-old daughter in the police station, with city police looking on approvingly, because she had been picked up for drunkenness. The account does not say what kind of life had led her to drink, nor does it say

[3] The Detroit Free Press, Dec. 31, 1946, page 1.

whether the treatment induced more or less drinking. The whole episode would seem to make another drink imperative.

Adult crime was never more prevalent. It is, of course, the only possible outcome of increased juvenile delinquency. Almost never does an adult start on a career of crime. He is universally the fruit of the soil which nurtured him. The cost of crime in the United States is said to be as much as thirteen billion dollars annually. This is enough to really provide the good life to every child in America if it went for constructive uses. It makes the two and a half billions[4] spent for elementary and secondary education seem rather trivial.

Some communities are now granting more divorces than marriage licenses. This is in part an aftermath of war and its hasty marriages, but surely not altogether as simple as that. It seems to indicate that a great many people are finding life unsatisfactory and are seeking a way out. The mate is often the scapegoat for more basic dissatisfactions.

This list could be greatly extended if it were necessary to make the point that, somewhere along the way, people have acquired patterns of living which do not work. Some may say that it was ever thus, but the figures do not support this contention.[5] One of my early recollections is of the San Francisco earthquake. I lived at that time on a farm in Michigan. The papers were full of the details for weeks, and my parents and their neighbors talked of little else. Our village sent its own small contribution of relief supplies. It seems hard now to realize that only about six hundred people lost their lives, and that San Francisco was not nearly so badly devastated as London

[4] "The Public and Education," published by the National Education Association, Washington, D.C., March 7, 1946.

[5] Again, see Chapter I in "Education and World Tragedy," by Jones, previously referred to.

or Rotterdam, not to mention Berlin or Hiroshima. Recently more people than that were shot down on the streets of Bombay, and the news hardly made page one. We have become inured to death and blood. We would need to be, in order that some of us might calmly discuss the pros and cons of war with Russia.

You may wonder what good can come from thus setting forth the ills of mankind, as we look forward to the latter half of our bloodiest century. Have we no virtues? Of course we have, but not enough; and we cannot make progress by just citing our virtues. I say "not enough" because the attitude of the man on the street is apprehensive, and this apprehension keeps him from seeking the good life, and turns him toward destructive thoughts and acts. It is here simply contended that all is not well, and the basic difficulty lies in patterns of thought and action laid down by the society in which man grows. It is my purpose, having pointed out the fact that all is not well, to seek basic causes, and to strive for suggestions as to how patterns might be laid down, as man is nurtured from the cradle, which will make life tenable—tenable not just for the few, but for every human being anywhere, who by being born has inherited the earth.

CHAPTER II

Some Common Assumptions of Education

We have seen from the previous statement that man as he goes through this life is too much ridden with fear and prejudice. Fear, being a most destructive emotion, makes man do many things that are against the best interests of his fellow men and in the long run against his own best interests.

Now we must consider how he comes to be this way, and whether there is anything that can be done about it. Do we have to go on in our destructive ways until we have destroyed each other? Or can our attention be turned toward ourselves for the betterment of our species? This has been the base of the hope we have held in religion, but the prospect of our all starting to practice religion seems remote. Our alternative seems to be that we must look to education in its broad sense to create a people able to continue to inhabit the earth.

So far as we now know, all that man is in habit and attitude, belief and prejudice, he has learned since he was born. There is nothing inherited by the newborn babe that decides whether he will be fearful or courageous, trusting or suspicious. These attitudes, then, must come from the society in which he grows up. This is not to deny the importance of inherited factors, but to doubt inherited attitudes.

The most important social factor for the very young

child is his parents and the other members of his family. If they regard him as something to do things *to* rather than *with*, and if they are determined to bend his personality to their wills, if they so treat him that he must fend for himself against them, this will have a profound influence upon him for the rest of his life. Indeed, throughout his whole development the atmosphere of the family probably has more to do with the kind of person he will become than any other one factor.

The child is likewise bent by all the other forces in his society. In modern times the movies have a great deal to do with establishing attitudes. The radio, the corner drugstore, playmates, the church, all contribute to the make-up of a human being.

We are particularly interested here, however, in the part played by the school in making fearful, prejudiced people. It is true, as has been shown, that the school does not carry the entire responsibility for the kind of people our society develops. But it is one institution that gets an opportunity to influence all people. The parents, who do not do too well by their children, all went to school at one time or another. The public school is the one place where we pool our funds and try to set up an institution that will redound to the benefit of all. Because it is so inclusive and because it is tax supported, it becomes the one institution which we should be able to modify. Since it is our major social effort to develop people who are competent to meet life adequately, to give more than they take, and to be capable of good citizenship in its largest social sense, the school must bear a major part of the responsibility for these outcomes. It might be profitable, then, for us to consider some of the major assumptions upon which our teachers and educators have so far acted and still too often do act.

These assumptions have been with us so long and are so firmly grounded in tradition that they have virtually become axioms to us. They are hard for us to dig out because they are so deeply embedded. We have believed them so long that we scarcely know we believe them. A few of these axioms or assumptions which I have been able to isolate are listed below.

It is not intended here to imply that all teachers and school administrators proceed on these assumptions. Many teachers have intuitively operated contrary to them, because of their high regard for human values, and because of the success they have achieved by this regard. The assumptions listed below are merely the usual, and not by any means the universal, bases for operation. They are so common, however, that they have succeeded in laying down too many of our present adult patterns.

1. *We assume that the child goes to school to acquire knowledge, and that knowledge is something which has existed for a long time and is handed down on authority.* Perhaps this goes far back to tribal days before the time of written records, when the elder who represented authority told the young what was known of human history. This assumption implies that knowledge exists before learning can begin.

Learning, then, under this assumption becomes a matter of acquisition and acceptance. We acquire that which is set out to be learned, and we do not question its validity because we have it on authority. These things which are set out to be learned become the essentials. They are essential because somebody thinks they are. When something is set out by a person in authority to be learned, it then becomes an absolute good.

Since knowledge is something handed down on authority and exists before learning can begin, it gives rise to many of the trappings of our education. The ordinary textbook is a good example of this. The textbook not only sets out what is to be learned, but it also eliminates that which is not to be learned. This brings comfort to the teacher, who like all of us, is a person of specialized and limited knowledge and understanding, because if the teacher can confine his efforts to the textbook, then he can maintain his pose as an authority.

2. *We assume that subject matter taken on authority is educative in itself*. This means that when the acquisition referred to above has been accomplished, the person almost automatically becomes educated. If this assumption is true, then the task of the teacher becomes that of seeing to it that acquisition takes place. Since such a fine thing as an education is to be the outcome, almost any method is justifiable. If the student will not acquire, then it becomes the teacher's business to see to it that he does. This often if not usually calls for coercion of one sort or another. This coercion may be brutal and overt, or it may be insidiously sweet. What we do to people in the process does not greatly matter, because the subject matter set out to be learned is an absolute good, and once it is learned the learner will be educated.

3. *We assume that the best way to set out subject matter is in unassociated fragments or parcels*. It may be that we really do not believe this, but we proceed as though we do. The heritage which we attempt to impart exists as a whole—the language, the mathematics, the science, the history are all intermingled to make a whole. Yet we take them apart and teach each one of them as something by itself. The English teacher cares very little what the student thinks about Columbus as long as he gets his phrases and clauses right. The history teacher concerns himself very little with the proper use of the language so long as

his essential facts of history are remembered. The mathematics teacher has so far departed from the concretions which give rise to numbers that he is virtually in a world by himself. If there is ever any process of putting these separate items back together where they were in the beginning, it has to be done by the learner. The learner's ability to synthesize is certain to be blunted by the analytical nature of this type of education.

This process not only does not use synthesis, but it "sets" the learner in the opposite direction.

Perhaps this analytical parcelling of the absolute goods comes from the notion that the mind is something separate from the body, and further, that the mind itself is divided into compartments. We do certain things in school which are supposed to train our will power, others to train our reasoning power or our memory, as though these functions were separate and resided in particular parts of the brain.

In much the same manner, we parcel or classify people as well as subject matter. We say all twelve-year-olds are the same and should learn the same things. They should make progress en masse. The only time we recognize growth is in May or June when most children are promoted at once. Others are told that they will have to do their growing over again.

4. *We assume that a fragment or parcel of subject matter is the same to the learner as to the teacher.* Thus we demand that children see the same significances in facts as we do. If I, as teacher, extract certain meanings out of an object or idea, I see no reason why a child should not extract the same meanings. That which is set out to be learned is absolute and therefore cannot have more than one meaning. So we say to children, "You heard what I

said, didn't you?" or, "You can see, can't you?" The teacher's bag of tricks has many such expressions in it.

Similarly, we assume that an object or fact, fragment or parcel, is the same to one learner as it is to another. That is, we can expect all the members of a class to learn the same thing, and to extract the same meaning from it. This assumption is really basic to all education that deals with subject matter which is "set out to be learned." It is implied in all of our factual examinations, our reliance on textbooks, and our efforts to educate large similar groups en masse. Later on, the bearing of this assumption will be more clearly shown.

5. *We assume that education is supplementary to and preparatory to life, not life itself.* The child is constantly in the process of preparing for something. He does not know quite what it is that he is preparing for, and the teacher is often ill-equipped to help him to know. Perhaps this comes from the situation which existed a century or more ago, when people lived in a world that was more concrete, and the school supplemented these concretions by furnishing the abstractions. Now we seem to be furnishing abstractions for concretions which no longer exist. To illustrate, we begin to teach a child to read when he is six years old. The abstract printed page has no relationship to any experience or need felt by most six-year-old children, but we know that sometime he will need to know how to read, and so we try to teach it to him regardless of his readiness or his purpose and without any relationship to the life which he is presently leading.

Since education is supplementary and preparatory, we build school buildings designed to shut out life so that the child can give complete attention to our abstractions or tools for conveying these abstractions, to books, blackboards, and chalk. The windows of the classroom are often purposely built high so that the child cannot look out of them and be distracted. The whole atmosphere of the place where education goes on is exclusive and forbidding in its nature. We build our colleges out in isolated places where the world will not intrude. We segregate the most similar ones together, where they cannot learn from different kinds of people. Often we do not let them associate even with their own kind, unless they are also of the same sex. Perhaps the place where a visitor from another country could learn the least about life in America would be on a typical college campus or, for that matter, in a typical American schoolroom.

All of this isolation is consistent with the assumption that children are not living but are preparing for life, that knowledge set out to be learned can be acquired and kept in cold storage, that it is of no use now but will come in handy sometime.

6. *We assume that since education is not present living, it has no social aspects.* When a child is acquiring the abstractions which have been set out for him, all social intercourse is eliminated. He works by himself, at a desk, as much alone as though he were not surrounded by many other social beings. Of course we have some trouble keeping him from being social, and to the extent that he is social we regard him as an undesirable student. The one who pays the least attention to the fact that he is surrounded by other social beings is the one we value most. Particularly undesirable is the one who either gives help to or receives help from another social being.

The unsocial character of what goes on in school gives rise to competition as a way of life. When one works by himself and does not give or receive help, the need to beat the other fellow who is working by himself at a similar task is sure to be felt. Indeed, it is the only recourse left

The idea of beating the other fellow is the opposite of helping him, and when helping is inhibited, competition is certain to take its place. It is implicit in the assumption.

7. *We assume that the teacher can and should furnish the purpose needed for the acquiring of knowledge.* This necessarily goes along with the idea that the teacher shall decide what is to be taught. If knowledge is something handed down on authority then the question as to whether the student has purpose with regard to it is unimportant. The student not only has his knowledge set out for him, but at the same time he is provided with somebody else's purposes and goals. Since this knowledge is absolute and essential, the question as to whether the student is interested in it or not becomes unimportant. The teacher sometimes forgets that if he is going to furnish the subject matter and the purpose he must also assume all responsibility. He often rails against his students because they do not assume responsibility for his purposes. If the teacher forgets to make an assignment, the student is free and has no responsibility to pursue learning.

Getting students to work motivated by somebody else's purpose is something of a task. In order to make students learn what they would not learn of their own accord, teachers have invented all kinds of extrinsic rewards and punishments. This is, in part, the basis for our system of giving good and bad grades, stars, and medals, and for our honor societies. They are devised to get students to do things which they would not otherwise do, and in which they see little or no value. The motive is fear of failure and the accompanying social pressures that go with failure. The reward is the chance to feel superior to somebody else.

8. *We assume that working on tasks devoid of purpose or interest is good discipline.* We somehow have a notion

that working at disagreeable tasks will make people like them and be willing to do them later in life. We assume that making a child conform to the classroom atmosphere which we have established will make him want to conform when he gets out of school. We give our best grades and honors to our most submissive people, presumably on the assumption that submissive people are the best people.

There seems to be an idea among adults that children are naturally perverse and must be coerced, that it is our function as adults to make them conform to habits and procedures which we hold good. We start to do things to children (coerce them) in the cradle on the assumption that they will not do good unless we make them do it, and that making them do it is good discipline.

We assume that when a child has been submissive he has assumed responsibility. If we assign a lesson to be studied at home and the child studies it, we say that he is very responsible. We say that he is a good citizen. We like to feel that we teach responsibility because creating responsible citizens is a charge that has been put upon us by society.

9. *We assume that the answer to the problem is more important than the process.* In the abstract world which is the school we confront our pupils with a mass of synthetic problems which they are asked to solve. If the student gets the right answer we are often satisfied. He probably cares nothing about how much imaginary carpet it takes to cover a hypothetical floor, but if he comes up with the right answer he gets a reward. We seem to assume that this theoretical problem is the same to him as a real one and that he has been through a problem-solving situation. We assume that it contains the elements of cut-and-try, failure and revision. But the child, with his eye on the answer (to get the teacher off his back) often asks

the absurd question, "Shall I multiply or divide?" As long as he can ask this question, he has no concept of the process.

10. *We assume that it is more important to measure what has been learned than it is to learn.* The typical recitation where the student recites what has been read in a book is essentially an evaluative process. Since much of the time in school is spent in recitation we are really using our time evaluating what has been learned somewhere else. In our programs of testing and examining we are deceived by a student's ability to return abstractions to us, and we call it evidence of learning. We seem to assume that evaluation is an outside process—that is, that a person can truly evaluate somebody else, and supposedly, if he himself is to be evaluated, that it should be done by somebody else. Evaluation of what has been done hence becomes more important than doing, because more time is devoted to it.

These are at least some of the assumptions under which the school attempts to build people who will be courageous, resourceful, responsible, and adequate. We seem not too much disturbed by the fact that our students portray an increasing attitude of indifference to us as we go along.

The little child who enters school is infinitely curious, and he is willing, as a rule, to give adult proposals a trial. This curiosity, at least with regard to what is set out to be learned, gradually disappears. In the place of curiosity we accumulate resistance. It gradually comes about that scarcely any adult proposal receives consideration. Whatever it is we propose to set out for him, he is sure he wants none of it. Throughout his educational career, in many cases, he skips school as often as he dares. The joy of the child when school closes in the spring and his sorrow when it opens in September is part of our regular way of life. When he reaches the legal age for quitting school he joyfully departs and does not even take his pencil and paper with him. He must proceed as he is, and use the patterns which he has established. If he has acquired habits of fear and coercion, if his learning is vague and disassociated, if his attitude toward people is one of suspicion, that is what he must use to meet the world. For if he has not had living experience in school, his departure from it will indeed be a "commencement," whether it is blessed by a ceremony and a diploma or not. If he has not lived in school, he will have to commence to live outside, as best he can. He can only be co-operative and social to the extent that by this time he has learned to be.

CHAPTER III

The Hanover Institute Demonstrations in Perception

Our opinions, assumptions, and prejudices must come from what we believe about ourselves, the people around us, and the world in which we live. It may be that some of these assumptions are wrong. Perhaps the best place to study them is to consider what comes to our eyes. The eye is not our only source of information, but it is certainly our most important one, and this is particularly true when we consider the surroundings that are too far from us to touch. If we can understand the nature of what we see, we will know much more about what we think, feel, and hold as attitude.

In Chapter II we have dealt with some of the common practices in education. But all education has to work through perception of one kind or another. How perception is induced, and where it comes from, is of vital importance to educators. Perception is their stock-in-trade. If we understood perception fully, we might then learn to work in keeping with the laws which govern it. This of course applies to all perception, whether visually or otherwise induced. If any one of the assumptions in Chapter II is wrong, it is wrong because it violates what we know about the nature of what is real as revealed through a better understanding of perception.

The Hanover Institute has some extremely interesting and important demonstrations constructed in its laboratories that deal with the nature of our visual perceptions. They seem the more important because they are physical and factual; that is, you and I can sit down beside them, work them ourselves, and draw our own conclusions from them. They furnish laboratory proofs of a number of visual facts which some of us have felt were true, but which we held only as opinions. They demonstrate what for long has been in the realm of conjecture and speculation.

WHERE DOES WHAT WE SEE COME FROM?

The first of these demonstrations serves to show that *we do not get our perceptions from the things around us, but that the perceptions come from us.* Since they do not come from the immediate environment (the present), and obviously cannot come from the future, they must come from the past. If they come from the past, they must be based on *experience.*

The demonstration is as follows: Let us assume that you are the person going through the demonstration for the first time. You are presented with three separate peepholes about the size of the pupil of the eye. You are asked to look through these holes in turn. The material back of the holes is well lighted. In each case you see a cube, with its three dimensions and its square sides. The three cubes look substantially the same. All appear to be about the same distance away. (See Figure A.)

Then you are permitted to look behind the boards through which the peepholes were cut. When you do this, you see that one of the holes really has a wire cube behind it. Another, however, has a drawing on a plane, with scarcely any of the lines running parallel. The third is a number of strings stretched between wires running away from the eye. (See Figure B.)

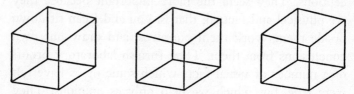

Figure A.   This is what we saw when we looked through each peephole in succession. The cubes are substantially the same. Each has three dimensions, and each has rectilinear sides.

Neither of the latter two looks anything at all like a cube when viewed from behind the scenes. And yet the thing perceived in each case was a cube. Even after you know what is behind the scene, if you look through the peepholes again you still see cubes.

The peephole served the purpose of limiting your vision to one eye and of establishing a point of view. It did nothing to modify the material viewed. We say that one was a cube and the others were not because that one remained a cube no matter which way it was viewed, or when. The others were cubes from one point of view, but not from any other.

In life we look mostly through a peephole, because we take quick looks from where we are, and make judgments. Often there is little relationship between the perception and the external object from which the stimulus came. The flat drawing and the strings on wires were as truly cubes to us as the one which remained a cube no matter which way we looked at it.

This means that the external material is not a cube until we call it one, and then it is a cube regardless of what its size, shape, and position may be. Therefore, the things

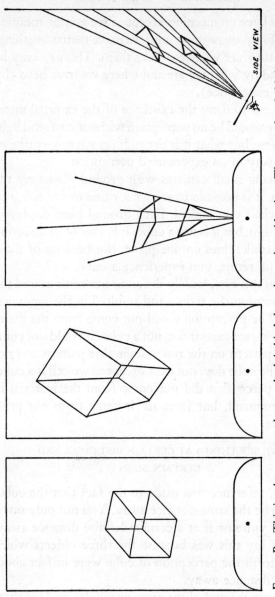

FIGURE B. This is what we see when we look behind the scenes. The one at the left is a cube made of wires. The center one is a drawing on a flat surface. The third is a set of wires with strings on them. This latter one is also shown in a side view. The second and third ones do not resemble cubes in any regard. They lack rectilinear sides and one of them lacks three dimensions.

around us have no meaning except as we ascribe meaning to them. They are nothing until we make them something, and then they are what we make them. This can only be determined by what we are and where we have been (by our prior experience).

This is not to deny the existence of the external material. There would be no perception without it to send light stimuli to us; but what it is depends on what we make of it, in the way of an experienced perception.

By moving small cameras with ground glass over the peepholes, it is possible to see what came to the retina of the eye when you looked. Each ground glass displays a similar design, but it is not a cube. It is a set of intersecting and nonparallel lines on one plane. But because of those lines on the retina, you experience a cube.

Thus, in this case, widely different materials caused the same pattern on the retina, and resulted in the same perception. The perception could not come from the material, since in two cases it was not a cube. It could not come from the pattern on the retina since that pattern was not a cube. The cube does not exist except as we call it a cube; and that perception did not come from the material in our environment, but from us. It came from our prior experience.

WE SEE THINGS AT CERTAIN DISTANCES AND CERTAIN SIZES

Earlier, reference was made to the fact that the cubes appear to be the same distance away. You not only saw a cube, but you saw it at a certain definite distance away. You may say this was because the three objects which brought forth the perception of cube were in fact about the same distance away.

Look now through three more peepholes, and see three more cubes each about the same distance away. Then look behind the boards. You will see that while the material there is similar to that in the first demonstration, the wire cube is one foot from the peephole, the plane with lines is three feet away, and the strings on wires are eight feet away. Yet you ascribed the same distance to all of them. You also ascribed a certain direction to them, and this, through the use of mirrors, can be equally false.

Therefore you not only have falsely experienced the perception of a cube, but you have ascribed false distance and false position with relation to yourself. This means that when we receive a stimulus pattern we not only say what it is (usually about right but not always) but we give it a distance from us and a position or direction. The object cannot be called a cube without also being identified in our minds with a size, distance, and direction. These ideas are as truly ascribed (given by past experience) as the name we gave it. And one or all of these can be wrong.

So we go through life receiving stimulus patterns and rightly or wrongly calling them objects and placing them in relation to ourselves. The name and position we give to the object do not lie in the objects themselves, but in what we ascribe to them out of our past experience. No two people can do the same ascribing, because no two people can bring the same experiential background to the task. So what we call reality lies in each unique background, and not in the objects which send the light rays. The only reality we can experience is what we make of the objects around us, and is always unique for each of us.

WERE YOU TRICKED?

But you say that we tricked you, because we put objects behind the peepholes which we knew would lead you to see cubes, and if a cat had been behind one of them, you would not have seen a cube. This is true, but nature is always putting things before you which lead you to experience perceptions which differ from what is viewed. The difference between what is seen in nature and the "trickery" of the cube experiment is only one of degree. We are not often (but still occasionally) so completely "tricked." If your perceptions are too far removed from the object sending the light, catastrophe may result, as in the following experience.

Recently, while driving along a road, I came up behind another car which I wanted to pass. I pulled over to the left, and saw another car in the distance. To me, it was a receding car, so I had nothing to fear from it. When I got alongside the car I wanted to pass, I looked again and saw that my first perception had been wrong, that it was an approaching car, and that I barely had time to throw on the brakes and get behind the car I was attempting to pass. If I had persisted in my first diagnosis, dire consequences would have resulted.

In another circumstance, that car would always have been a receding car to me, a rear end instead of a front. If I had seen the car out the window of my office it would not have mattered which I thought it was. Ordinarily I never would have had to revise my diagnosis, and reality for me would have been what I first thought it was. This is happening to us all the time, mostly (but not always) in cases which do not greatly matter. Nobody knows how many such false perceptions one experiences when he casually views the general scene.

WE GET MANY DIFFERENT CLUES ABOUT OUR SURROUNDINGS

"But," you say, "I don't go through life looking through peepholes. I have many ways by which I can determine what is really out there."

That is true. First, you have two eyes instead of one, so that you automatically get two stimulus patterns, from slightly different points of view, making the stimulus patterns slightly different. We say that gives you a better slant on things, although it works only on near objects. When viewing a distant scene the value of having two eyes becomes negligible.

You have many other clues which you use because you have found them helpful. One of these clues is size. The larger an object, without other clues, the nearer it appears. Another is brightness. You expect faraway objects to be less bright, so you think the dimmer object is farther away. Another is overlay. If the tree outside my window blots out part of the house which is also out there, I see the tree nearer than the house. If the house blots out part of the tree, I see the house nearer than the tree.

Another phenomenon which you make use of in locating objects in your world is parallax. Parallax is the movement of objects in the foreground in relation to those in the background when we move. When you move your head sidewise, the nearer objects seem to move. We are always moving back and forth to get a better slant on things. This apparent movement of nearer objects as we move is one of our most useful clues. The normal movement involved in walking gives us continuous parallax clues.

These are constantly referred to as clues, because they do not tell us the nature of an object or its location, but they give us indications on which we make decisions. We add them all together and the result is our best guess at the nature and location of our environment. So we never can be absolute about it—all we ever have is an estimate of what is there, as a sort of statistical average of a good many clues. The estimate is *what we make of it* after we receive

the stimulus. What we make it is the only workable reality in the whole proposition. We make it what we must
make it on the basis of our past experience. We have an
inclination to make it what we want it to be, so that it con-
forms with the familiarity of our experience and with our
purpose. The fact that I wanted the car, in the earlier
illustration, to be a receding one probably had something
to do with my seeing it that way.

Most of us are inclined to trust our clues too much;
many of us trust them implicitly, so that we say that what
we get from sight and our surroundings correspond, i.e.,
they are identical. So we come to regard an object as an
absolute, that is, the same to you as it is to me. Perhaps the
reason we do this is because our clues *are* very good, and
so we pronounce them perfect.

OUR CLUES ARE UNRELIABLE

By laboratory demonstration it is possible to show that
not one of the clues we use is to be trusted absolutely. Our
next experiment has to do with the trustworthiness of size
and brightness in establishing distance; for we *do* have to
know how far an object is from us if we are going to use
it, and we *do* ascribe distance on the basis of such clues
as we have.

The experiment consists of two rubber balloons, inflated to the same size and lighted from above, and being
so set up that you can mechanically, from some distance
away, vary the size (putting in or letting out air) and
brightness (varying the current which enters the bulbs
above the balloons). The room is darkened, to reduce the
number of other clues available. The balloons are side by
side, that is, they are the same distance from you. As you
make one larger and the other smaller, the larger one appears to come toward you, the smaller one to recede. If

you leave them the same size but make one brighter and the other dimmer, the brighter one seems to come nearer, the dimmer one to recede. If you make one both bigger and brighter, the feeling of approach is even greater. All the time the two balloons are of course the same distance away. So the clues of bigness and brightness for determining distance are both unreliable. They will be substantially correct most of the time, so we use them. They are not to be trusted completely.

In like manner, by simple devices it is possible to show that neither overlay nor parallax is to be trusted. If we make the object farther away move more than the near one, it appears nearer. If we cut a corner out of a playing card and line it up with a green square much farther back, so that in our field of vision the green square exactly fits the corner cut away, the green square will appear near, the playing card far away.

WHAT IS AN ILLUSION?

You may want to say at this stage that these demonstrations are optical illusions, and that psychologists have cast illusions outside reality. It would appear that since our perception is an adding up of our clues to approach correspondence with the outside world, *but that they never do quite correspond*, therefore we can say that we are constantly experiencing illusion to a degree. These demonstrations are only exaggerations to make a point. If we say that the only reality is our perception, then there is no such thing as an illusion; the perception merely varies more or less from the environment. The only thing in the whole sequence that matters is the perception, since that tells us what the object is to us. The functioning reality is what we make of it, not what started the sequence, and which we misinterpreted to a degree. To dis-

miss one of these misinterpretations as an illusion because
it is unusually different from the object which started the
chain of events is to place the importance on the object
(which may be of very little importance) instead of the
meaning extracted from the perception, which is all-
important, since it is the meaning which governs what
we do.

WE HAVE NO COMMON WORLD

All of this leads up to the following facts. Our perceptions do not come simply from the objects around us, but
from our past experience as functioning, purposive organisms. We take a large number of clues, none of which is
reliable, add them together, and make what we can of
them. All that this gives us is an estimate of our surroundings. It is never exactly right. It is never the same for different individuals. It is like a statistical average, a useful
device for making a prognosis, but always wrong in any
particular instance.

Since the perception is the usable reality, and since no
two organisms can make the same use of clues or bring
the same experiential background to bear, no two of us
can see alike. We have no common world. Each has his
own, to which he responds in his own way. Because our
forecasts usually approximate correctness, we make the
mistake of assuming they are perfect, and that we do have
a common world.

WHAT THEN IS REAL?

By this time you may be disturbed by what we have
been saying about reality, but this is just what we must be
clear about, for what is real to a person is of utmost importance to him. It is from a feeling of reality that we get
our sense of surety, and we must have that in order to

have confidence to do anything (to act). You have always felt that the objects around you were real, and have taken comfort from the thought that you knew what they were. Now I tell you that the only reality is a perception, located somewhere behind the eyes.

You make the point that the book before us on this desk is real. We both can see it is a book. We can pick it up and turn its pages. We can read it. We can put it back in another spot, and we both will change our position to it.

This seems sound. Certainly there is something on the desk which, since our backgrounds both have books in them, we both call a book. But instead of emphasizing what we know about it, let us look for a moment at what we do not know. Some of this may seem unimportant, may even weary you a bit. Its purpose is to show that we do not actually know as much about a book as is usually assumed, and that what we do know is subjective. It is to show that even a book lacks meaning in its own right, and is only what each of us makes it to be.

To begin with, we don't know how big it is, and we cannot know. We can measure its length, breadth, and thickness and get some idea in an abstract way. But the measurements are only approximations. Nobody ever measured anything exactly. Scientists know this and that is why they are always trying to invent finer instruments of measurement. They say an instrument is accurate down to one ten-thousandth of an inch, but never that it is accurate. When we put our finest measuring devices on it, all we get is an estimate of its length. It is like the estimate we make with our eyes, except that it is more accurate, although the one we make with our eyes usually has more value in use.

Measurements of distance are about as accurate as any device we have. But in measuring the distance to a star, we use light-years. If you heard that a certain star is 2,600 light-years away, and then learned that it is really 2,601 light-years away, you would not be impressed with the inaccuracy. Yet it is one whole light year wrong, and that is a distance beyond human understanding. Anyway, by this time, since both star and earth are moving, it is no longer that distance but some other.

This last thought applies equally to the book. If it were possible to measure it accurately, which it is not, it would not have the same measurement tomorrow. For it is made of molecules, which are escaping from it and, as it lies there on the desk, it is slowly disintegrating. It is returning to a state of disorder.

Whatever has been said about its size applies equally to its weight. With the finest weighing devices known to science, we could get an abstraction which would express (abstractly) a very close estimate of weight, but no scientist would claim that it was accurate. This abstraction would not be as useful to the average person as though he had "hefted" it. When we "heft" it we find out, nearly enough for our purposes, what it weighs, and that is all we care about. But it weighs a different amount to a healthy adult than to a two-year-old child.

In terms of use, even, it has no reality in its own right. I may see it as a block to hold the door open, or something in which to press flowers. You may see it as something to read or to throw at the dog. If I can't read, or if it is written in a foreign language, it is not something for me to read.

We must avoid giving the impression that there is nothing there on the desk. Certainly there is something there, and I can get a pretty good estimate of what it is (but never a perfect one). But it is something different to you than what it is to me, and therefore it has no reality or validity in its own right. It only has reality and validity as you and I assign them, and its only importance lies in what we make of it. The concept you and I have of it is all that really counts, and your concept is different from mine.

This concept came entirely from the past. I call it a book because I have book experience. If I had no book experience, I would not call it a book. So whatever we have that is real in the whole situation comes from each of us (our past as experiencing organisms), and varies with each of us.

WE ACT ON OUR PERCEPTIONS

But why should we say the perception of book is real and the object which sent the light rays to us is not? It is because the perception (not the object) is a directive for action. What we do is on the basis of the perception, not on the basis of the object. The book does not matter to me, may not even be observed, unless I do something with it or about it. What I do depends upon what my experience and purpose brought to the situation.

Since the perception, not the object, is a directive for action, it is important that I get as accurate an estimate as possible; otherwise my actions will be too much in conflict with my surroundings. My actions are always at variance with my surroundings to a degree, and when this becomes too great, failure is the result. Then I have to make a new forecast on the basis of added information, and try again. If my estimate is too bad and my environment too obstructive, my purposes are defeated and I become frustrated. Whenever this occurs I seek to overcome it by one response or another. I may become aggressive and try force, or I may withdraw from the situation. If there is not too much feeling involved in the frustration, I may make a new estimate and try again.

It is easy to demonstrate the fact that a bad diagnosis results in faulty action. This often happens to each of us, usually in unimportant situations. It is the basis for camouflage, burlap tanks, inflated rubber guns, etc., used in warfare. Lookout Mountain was "defended" by the Confederates for weeks by wooden guns. All of these devices are intended to induce the enemy to faulty action based on wrong prognosis and faulty perception.

The fact that perception is a directive for action is demonstrated in the laboratories of The Hanover Institute by what is called the distorted room. It is a box with one side open, so that we can look into it. The right side is small, the left side large, so that the floor, back, and ceiling have to slant away from the right side, to meet the left. The floor therefore slants down to the left, the ceiling up to the left, and the back away to the left. The right-hand corners are therefore much nearer than the left-hand corners. (See Figure C.)

A metal ball hangs near the ceiling in the left-hand corner, and a similar one hangs in the corresponding right-hand corner.

Now you put on a pair of glasses which shortens the left side, and you see the room as rectangular.[1] You are asked to touch the left-hand ball with a stick. You know the ball is far away, but you put the sick where it *appears* to be. This does not touch the ball, so you extend the stick farther and farther until you finally touch the ball. Now

[1] The effect of the glasses is as follows: When you look at the room with either eye alone it appears rectilinear, because it is so built that the uniocular clues are similar to those that you get from a rectilinear room. The effect of the glasses is to give you binocular clues that are similar to those that you get from a rectilinear room. These two sets of false clues, supplementing each other, increase your sense of surety that your false impression is a true one.

Figure C. This is a drawing of the distorted room. It does not show the distortion fully, because the back left corner does not appear to be far enough away from us. The reason for this is that there are so many things built into the room which violate the usual rules of perspective. For example, consider the two back windows. If they were the same size, the left one should look smaller than the right one, because it is farther away. It is actually larger, and when drawn larger, the left corner refuses to go back where it belongs. In order to realize how far away the back left corner is, we have to have the plan view, which is a horizontal cross section of the room. For the experiment, the observer is placed nearer the right wall than the left one.

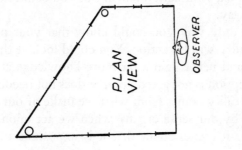

PLAN
VIEW

OBSERVER

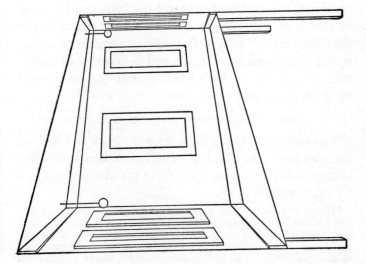

you are asked to touch the other ball quickly. You far overreach it and hit the back wall with the stick. Finally you withdraw the stick enough to touch the right-hand ball. (See Figure D.)

When you saw the room through the glasses, all square, you knew intellectually that the room was not that way. It was the present perception on which you acted. That was your present reality. Because the perception didn't fit the box, your action failed. But you could not act any other way.

The only way you could know that your perception was faulty was by action. You could look at the box for hours and never gain a bit more knowledge about it. If a perception is not acted upon, it does not become important. Reality comes from what we make of our clues, received by our sense organs, when we act upon them.

Thus it comes about that it is impossible to consider any environmental matter apart from the experiencing organism. It is invalid if we leave the "you and I" out of it. That is why we say that external objects lack reality in their own right.[2] They only attain importance when assigned characteristics, distance, and position by an experiencing organism. And what the organism assigns them to be comes from past experience.

ABOUT THE ABSTRACT AND THE CONCRETE

You may want to ask then, what the book is. Until we act with regard to it, it is an abstraction. It is a statistical average made by me on the basis of my clues interpreted by my experience.

[2] It may be necessary here to repeat that this is no denial of the existence of the viewed object. Something is there, and we have a pretty good estimate as to what it is. There would be no perception but for the object, but for the light rays coming from it and impinging on our sense organs. What it is, functionally, however, comes from us and does not reside in the object itself.

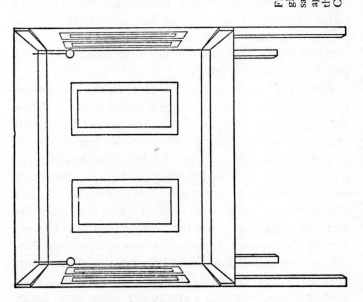

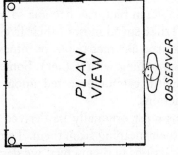

PLAN
VIEW

OBSERVER

FIGURE D. This is the distorted room as it appears with the glasses. Note that the back left corner appears to be the same distance away as the back right one. The back windows appear to be the same size. In the plan view, note that while the observer is actually to the right of the center (see Figure C) he seems to be in the center.

We make much use of abstractions. The written word "book" will serve almost as well to us who have knowledge of the written language as the object on the table. But we carry abstractions much further. Higher mathematics is a good illustration. You and I, not being highly trained in mathematics, can no more understand the symbols of higher mathematics than we can Chinese characters. Some people, in fact, can become so involved in abstractions that they spend most of their lives among them. A symbol, like the abstract book, becomes a concretion when we do something with it (act). Some symbols, like the written word, cannot be acted upon and therefore remain abstractions.

Abstractions must originally be derived from concretions and get their meaning from them. To the extent that we value abstractions in themselves, we depart from reality. For example, those who live almost entirely in a world of books depart from reality in that they fail to gain experience in "how to do," and become increasingly incapable of action. They are not ones with whom we would choose to be shipwrecked.

Abstractions kept reasonably close to the concretions from which they are derived are useful as tools. When we assign them reality in themselves, we confuse a tool with what we are making with the tool. The means becomes the end. The tail wags the dog. That is what happens when we teach a whole class of children concerning an object in their environment as though the object (the abstraction) were the same to all of them, and that it has absolute value apart from the persons involved. We are leaving the experiencing organism out of it, and the specific or specialized abstraction becomes the all-important factor. We are even further from reality when we use only written symbols on such a group. For while book, letter, and cipher are all abstractions, letter and cipher are further from reality because we cannot act with regard to them, while we can act with regard to the book. The book *can* become concrete.

We use the term "concrete" as the opposite of "abstract." We are being concrete when we act in regard to any object. Action is impossible without including the person (the experiencing organism). So we are really concrete only when the point of view of the person is included. To return to a previous example, the book is an abstraction, but it becomes concrete when it is taken in relation to the experiencing organism. This is particularly true if we use it (act with regard to it). If we block a door open with it, we have involved the person and the book in an act.

We have said that our perception consists of a sort of statistical average of all of our clues with regard to our surroundings. A statistical average of anything is an abstraction, and it is always wrong to a degree. At any rate it could only be right once in an infinite number of cases, and this is too small a chance to be useful. One of the best known statistical averages is the life-expectancy table used by insurance companies to predict income and costs. It is a useful and necessary abstraction, but it is never right in any particular case. It is near enough right to be useful, but always wrong. So our statistical average of our clues is always wrong, and our perceptions are always at variance with our surroundings, but usually near enough to be useful.

WE LIKE TO FEEL SURE

From the nearness of our perception to our surroundings we get our sense of surety. The more clues we have, the surer we feel. That is why we act more surely in the

daytime that we do at night. Whenever we get conflicting clues, we lose surety, and if there are too many of
these, we lose our capacity to act. The surroundings are
as reliable as ever, but our perception, which is all that
we can have, is confused. Conflicting clues can push us
to abnormality. Since perception comes entirely from the
past, it is possible to ascribe anything we desire to the
clues we receive. When we ascribe what we want to without regard to our surroundings, because our surroundings
are unsatisfactory to us, we are said to have departed from
reality (become insane). Probably we have not departed
from reality, if perception is reality, but have ceased to
use our clues and our perceptions have lost all similarity
to our surroundings.

When the person viewing the book and the book are
both taken into account, the book also has a certain distance and direction. This is essential to action. It is as
much a part of the total as are the weight and size of the
book. A common ungrammatical statement is "Give me
that there book," or "This here wrench is too small." We
tell people who say this that it is incorrect and they should
say, "Give me that book." But the expression is necessary
to include not only the object (that) but its position from
the person (there). When we insist on leaving the "there"
out of it, we are trying to get the person out, and leave
only the abstraction. We need two new words in our
language—"thatthere" and "thishere." Thus we would
automatically include the viewing person, which is necessary in order to be concrete.

SCIENTISTS TRY TO LEAVE OUT THE VIEWING PERSON

Scientists are devoted to the task of trying more and
more exactly to find out what is actually in the surroundings, so that these surroundings can be put to use. They

try to get measurements so fine that objects will be the same to you as to me. Now they are trying to use light waves, since they are supposed to be more absolute, in place of inches, centimeters, etc. They are trying to take the viewing organism out of the picture. They have succeeded to a remarkable degree in highly specialized instances. But they never quite succeed for the man in the street. By their methods they may invent a radio, for example, and the man in the street may carry a portable one with him. But he goes on trusting his old clues and including himself in every situation. The scientists make brief and difficult forays into the objective world and bring back a radio or an atomic bomb, but you and I do not go along with them. The big question remains, "What does it mean to us?" "What can *we* do with it?" The scientist comes back to us, too, for when he steps out of his laboratory to go to lunch, he does it just the way you and I do, with all his own purposes, experiences, and prejudices in full flower.

WE SELECT WHAT WE CHOOSE TO SEE

We do some interesting things with the perceptions which come to us. To begin with, we do not pay attention to all of them, or even a good fraction of them. We select the coincidences in nature which we choose to register. Given the same scene, or nearly so, no two people pay attention to the same factors in it.

Besides, we have a habit of assuming that similar things are alike. This is our effort to classify things. If we can say that a certain group of objects are the same, we don't have to deal with so many different kinds of objects. For example, if there are a large number of oak leaves before us, we put them all in one class, and each of us has his own idea of the standard oak leaf. In the laboratory it is

possible to show that different people carry different no-
tions as to the size of an oak leaf. Some of us make them
large, some small, but of course there is no such thing in
nature as a standard oak leaf. Nature never repeats or
standardizes. We standardize and classify (make statistical averages) because it increases the chance that our
prognosis will be reasonably correct. If there were no
observer or viewing person, there would be no classifica-
tions, because there would be no need for them.

Because we have found it so from experience, we tend
to say that similar things are identical, and we tend to put
together those things which we have associated together
before. This is one of the ways we get to see depth, or
perspective. If I see two telegraph poles, one shorter than
the other, in the right position, I assume they are the same
length, and that since they are the same length, one must
be farther away than the other. Without the tendency to
assume that they are the same length, they would appear
the same distance away, and I would miss the experience
of depth or perspective.

WHY DO WE SELECT WHAT WE DO?

Now you may want to raise the question as to why a
person selects what he does to pay attention to out of his
surroundings, and why he classifies them in his own way.
It is easy to show that no two persons do this alike. We
have said that we bring our past experience to bear upon
it, but this does not seem to be adequate to account for
the whole performance. In any ordinary scene, we have
past experience with practically everything in it, but we
do not elect to pay attention to everything. Our selection
therefore must be based on something in addition to
experience.

It apparently is a combination of past experience and

what we call purpose. The human being is a purposive creature. The drives necessary to survival, food, sex, etc., are fairly simple. But they seem to be only part of the purpose of the total organism, which has value at the core of it.

Valueful purpose is not as easy to demonstrate in a laboratory as is the nature of perception. But it can be conclusively demonstrated by the fact cited above, that the selective nature of perception cannot be accounted for in any other way. This is common and respectable scientific procedure. No one has ever seen an electron, but the characteristics of matter under certain conditions cannot be accounted for in any other way, so we accept their existence. In fact, no one questions their existence any more than he does those things which he can see.

We know that in prenatal life we get eyes before there is anything to see, feet before there is any walking to be done. The needs of the postnatal organism are foreseen and provided for so that the purpose of the organism may be carried out.

Perhaps purpose is the satisfaction of the ego, my demand for a place in the sun. This is relative and social, however, since if I were not surrounded by other people, it perhaps would be unimportant.

It might be that purpose is carried in the genes. A recent book, "What Is Life?" by Schroedinger, presents in understandable form the recent developments in scientific knowledge in the fields of physics and biology which make clear the nature of the gene and its importance, and shows that the gene is a molecule with a very special and permanent arrangement of atoms.[3] This set of atoms is the most permanent thing in the world. No two of us has the same arrangement. In going from one generation to

[3] "What Is Life?" by Erwin Schroedinger, Macmillan, 1945.

the next, it creates order out of disorder, whereas in all of the rest of the universe, atomic disorder is in progress. This personal and individual atomic arrangement (nobody else has one like ours) is called the codescript. It is both builder and plan. This may account, scientifically, for what we rather loosely call valueful purpose.

Purpose is not so hard to comprehend if we borrow from Kilpatrick and say that a thing *is* what it *does*. In this sense, he says, such things as habit and attitude are structure; that is, having acquired a habit, we are never again the same in how we act.[4] In this same sense, purpose can be part of our very structure.

At any rate, there is plenty of evidence for us to say that we are purposive organisms. When we take in our surroundings, we select from them, not at random, but in accordance with our past experience and our purposes. To a degree, we take out of the scene those elements which will forward our purposes and also those elements which we fear may frustrate our purposes. These are the only parts of the scene which attain functional reality, and they attain it only to the degree that they are taken account of and acted upon by a person. This he can only do in relation to his experience and purpose.

[4] "A Reconstructed Theory of the Educative Process," William H. Kilpatrick, Bureau of Publications, Teachers College, Columbia University, 1935.

CHAPTER IV

The Deeper Meaning of Vision

These experiments, then, throw new light on the visual process and its importance for behavior. It is the major tie that binds us to the outside world and tells us how to manage that outside world. But because of the individual nature of that tie, and because what is outside of us becomes real only in the light of the interpretation we put upon it, we become one with our environment. A whole man is all that his organism is in its interaction with his own unique environment. And vision is the connection between these two to tell how to behave. This makes the seeing process far more significant than we held it to be when we simply regarded the eye as a light-stimulus receiver.

To be sure, we have other avenues of perception. We hear, we smell, we feel, we taste. We also gain some knowledge of what lies outside us by muscular processes. Further study needs to be done in these areas, as well as in that of vision. Our other ways of knowing must be even less accurate—more prognostic—than vision. If we hear a peculiar noise outside the window, we are not content just to listen to it, but make an effort to bring its source into vision. When uncertain, we always try to look. Vision extends us into our environment much further than any of our other senses. Touch, taste, and smell are extremely limited as to distance. Hearing is also limited as compared to vision. We are probably most content with our perception when all of our ways of knowing are brought to bear on our surroundings, and when they support each other.

The whole man is one with his environment, connected by his means of securing his personal prognosis (his senses). Usual relationships are built into habit, and the usual world becomes the habitual world—the comfortable world. In all of this the sense most accurate and most relied upon is vision: "Seeing is believing." The eye becomes the chief avenue for establishing relationships upon which the organism depends for its security. Exactly where the organism leaves off and the environment begins then becomes an unimportant question, difficult to answer but not significant. The oneness of man and his surroundings is illustrated in exaggerated form when one views great beauty. The organism is transported and shares in the beauty.

When disarrangements occur in the established situations which have become habit, the person becomes upset. In the laboratory of The Hanover Institute this is shown in a number of ways. Some people become angry when they find that there are no cubes behind some of the peepholes. All are upset by the distorted room. When they try to reach the ball in the far left-hand corner with the stick and fall far short of it, they lose the sense of security usually accorded by vision. Some laugh, some swear, some become embarrassed. Old habits have failed, new relationships are called for. Knowing, intellectually, the distances involved is of almost no help. It is the visual connection upon which the organism acts, and when failure results, the organism reacts. The oneness of man and his environment has been disturbed.

Perhaps it would be worthwhile to describe another

experiment which very clearly demonstrates this point. It is a room with one wall missing, leaving a place for the observer. The room is all square, that is, its floor and ceiling are level and its three remaining walls make right angles to each other. The three walls, floor and ceiling are covered with oak leaves. Thus there are no clues in the room—just a box lined with leaves.

If you sit in a chair at the point of the missing wall, the room looks rectangular, although it is a little difficult to tell where one wall leaves off and another begins, because the oak leaves are all alike. Now if you put on a certain pair of glasses, the room immediately becomes distorted. The back wall is small and far away so that the floor has to slant up sharply and the ceiling slants down to meet it. The other two walls must slant accordingly. With other lenses, other distortions are possible, but this one will serve as an illustration.

The startling fact about this demonstration is not that the room can be distorted, but that it has such a profound effect on the one viewing it. One feels that his whole world has gone askew. This is accentuated if someone steps into the leaf room at this moment. You are sure that he will fall, and your whole organism, especially your stomach, reacts. I tried these lenses outside on the lawn, and found that to have the lawn slant sharply up, to have trees slant away, and all the other violations of what had become habit, was too much to be endured more than a few minutes.

This illustrates forcefully the intimate relation between body and surroundings, and what has happened to the body as the eye has served as connection and has reduced connection to habit. This probably accounts for seasickness. We do not become ill because the boat is moving, but because we cannot endure seeing water stand on edge. That is not what water is supposed to do. We cannot readily establish new oneness with this strange and seemingly unnatural relationship. We cannot easily let go of what has been built into habit.

When externality takes on new meaning, habit patterns become inadequate and must be revised. Some people do this readily, others have great difficulty in letting go what they have held. The capacity to become educated depends, it would seem, on the capacity of the individual to relinquish what he has held, and built new habit patterns in keeping with new environmental demands. This is quite a different concept of education from the one commonly held. We too often believe that education consists of the retention of abstractions largely gained by precept, either from lecture or book. But some of the most highly educated in this regard have the least capacity for dealing with actual life, for the abandonment of what has been built into habit and the construction of new responses to meet new needs. With such persons, the total self regresses when external arrangements become unfamiliar, and inadequacy results.

The most important factor in education then becomes the arrangements that the one to be educated makes with his environment through his senses, of which vision is the most important. This calls for the experiential approach. Perhaps it is the difference between knowing and knowing about. We can know about George Washington, for example, but that kind of knowing does not suffice for behavior; it is not the kind of knowing based on the oneness of the organism and the environment. We can only know Washington to the degree that there are some similarities between the conditions described and conditions with which we are familiar.

William H. Kilpatrick states the issue discussed above succinctly in the following statement:[1]

We who have studied these experiments in the light of broader thinking see other and more important bearings and this along two distinguishable lines. The first line is that the eye process of perception is, as a mere seeing process, of far wider application than appears to the uninitiated. This the artist, for example, sees. The second line is that the way the eye is shown in these experiments to act is a characteristic part of human behavior and therefore illustrative of each other line of behavior in the total organism's response; illustrative in fact of human behavior in certain of its most fundamental and inclusive aspects.

As an instance of this second line of application, these experiments show how the effort at behavior builds habits which are correlative of the conditions under which the appropriate behavior must go on if it is to succeed; and because the habits so built are correlative of the conditions under which that behavior went on, those habits may have to be changed when new conditions confront. In other words, education must go on under life conditions and does in fact come about through the effort to manage life. This is the foundation of the learning process as I myself understand it; and on this foundation must conscious education be appropriately built.

To go further along the line of this argument, logic is simply the best way of thinking we have yet been able to devise (and build into conscious habit) for managing the thought process. This definition of logic follows legitimately from the generalized conclusion from these eye experiments. In other words, these experiments lead logically to an experimental way of managing life, all of life.

This concept of vision leading thus to an experimental way of managing life throws new light on many of our present vexing problems. What does one of our diplomats see when he beholds a Russian? He sees what he has rele-

[1] In a letter to the author, January 13, 1947.

gated to habit in this area, and his usefulness to us in steering us toward a better world depends upon his ability to hold tentative his prior outlook and to build new responses when a changed world demands it. A 1925 attitude toward Russians as a stereotype will not suffice because Russia is no longer a weak, largely illiterate struggling people, but a world power to be lived with. And besides, the atom bomb has come to be among us. These facts call for new responses, and those who cannot make such new responses cannot serve us.

Again we are in our country trying to learn to live peaceably with people who are different from us. Since most of the people living in the United States are white of skin and Protestant in religion, we of the majority call different people our minorities. Since most of us grew up among people like ourselves, our stereotypes with regard to these minority peoples have little to do with what they are really like. We shall not learn to live with them democratically, ethically, in peace and understanding, until we learn to discard habitual patterns of thought in the light of new evidence, and build the needed new patterns into habit.

And so it is with all of the people of the world with whom we need communion. What do you see when you behold a banker, a union member, a Democrat, a Republican, a Communist, a Doctor of Philosophy, a Harvard Man, a woman, a piccolo player? Do your habit patterns suffice?

HOW CAN WE UNDERSTAND EACH OTHER?

From all this study of vision and behavior and habit we can now see what causes much of the difficulty in our relations with other human beings. No one can ever completely understand another person. This is true because we can never fully get the other person's point of view—that is, we can never be precisely where he is. Added to that, we cannot appreciate his own experiential background, nor his unique purposes.

Probably a good case can be made for the statement that we are naturally social beings. Not many of us, even in the days of the frontier, went off and lived by ourselves. If we do not desire the company of other human beings, it is doubtful that such an institution as the family could be perpetuated. But whether we are naturally social beings or not, we are immediately and continuously thrown in contact with other people, and perhaps the major task of life is adjustment to the fact that other people must also inhabit the earth.

In order to be effective social beings, we have to approach the other person's point of view. This can only be done through better and better communication. We have our mutual language when we are among our own people, and it helps greatly. But when it comes to establishing communion with strange peoples, which we grievously need in our small physical world, the difficulties are enormous.

Our current troubles with the Russians illustrate this. We have different experiential backgrounds, different purposes, we make different selections from our surroundings, and we do not even have the assistance of a common language. And yet the very survival of the two peoples in our one world rests upon the attainment of enough mutual understanding to be workable.

To attain complete communion with another human being would mean to occupy the same space he does and to have the same purposes and experience. This of course cannot be. But our success as social beings depends upon the degree to which we can attain communion with our fellow men. This calls for an understanding of the nature of practical reality, and why an object cannot be the same to you as it is to me. When I know this, I lose some of my cocksureness and begin to make allowance for other points of view, other drives, other purposes. I come to realize that my way cannot be your way, but that your way is as essential to you as mine is to me, and that we urgently need to invent, construct, devise new ways of gaining communion for the common weal.

I once heard a theologian discuss what St. Paul meant when he said, "The greatest of these is charity." Charity was interpreted to mean not almsgiving, as it is thought of in these times, but communion, experiential rapport, common consent and understanding. When we see the current need for better communication, communion, and rapport, it is easy to see why charity, thus defined, becomes "greatest."

CHAPTER V

Implications for Education

In the light of our assumptions about education, and the disclosures in Chapters III and IV, what can we then say about education? For educators cannot ignore the facts with regard to what is real, or how the person proceeds in his world of things and other people. If perceptions are directives for action, if reality is only achieved through action, and perceptions are never better than prognoses, the teacher must proceed in the light of these facts.

No claim to novelty can be made for the ideas which follow. Many people have known them for a long time. The prophets spoke in language based on these concepts. Such widely separated (in time) works as Aesop's Fables and Alice in Wonderland make use of them. There is no idea here expressed which cannot be found frequently in educational literature. The importance attached to them here comes from the fact that they are derived from demonstrations rather than from logic, intuition, and wisdom. The demonstrations should tend to satisfy even the scientists, who are loath to consider matters other than those which can be demonstrated by what they term the material world, and who require that such demonstrations be repeatable by others than the original demonstrator.

Further, every idea in this chapter is drawn more or less

directly from the demonstrations. It is perhaps true that in some cases I argue beyond the demonstrations themselves, on a train of thought started by them. This is my unique experience and background at work. It is implicit in what we have learned about perception that this should be so, and it is proper and consistent that it should be so. The items discussed here are *selected*, as we select in any perceptual situation, and the selection is part of the perception. I do not, for example, discuss teachers' salaries, an important educational topic, because I see no direct implication to them in the findings of The Hanover Institute.

WHAT IS ABSOLUTE?

The demonstrations tell us some interesting things about the nature of knowledge. Since all we ever get of what is outside us is a prognosis, what we know becomes an entirely personal matter. I can get my stimuli from the same objects as you do, but I cannot bring the same purpose and experience to them that you do. Therefore they are never the same to you as they are to me. We cannot eliminate the viewing person, else nothing would happen at all. Further, it cannot be the same to me tomorrow as it is today, because tomorrow my whole experiencing make-up will be somewhat different.

We can therefore set out things to be learned, but we can never get the same learning twice, and the knowledge (what we know) resulting will vary among individuals and from time to time.

This is destructive of the idea that knowledge is absolute. We have long taught school as though it were, and we cling to the idea of absolutes because we think it gives us surety.

Our absolutes in the world of knowledge become a little ridiculous when we look back at the absolutes held by others in the past. We assume that they did not have the answers, but that we have. We laugh now at the "know-it-alls" who said the world was flat; we are mildly amused at those who found all the answers in Newtonian physics or in Euclidian mathematics. We find it easy to believe that while their answers were wrong, ours are correct; not only that they are correct, but that they include all there is to know. The "know-it-alls" in the future will laugh at our conceit.

Perhaps the mistake of regarding knowledge as an absolute, and as existing before learning can begin, is best illustrated by our teaching of history. Surely there is nothing more uncertain than facts as to what happened yesterday, to say nothing of a hundred years ago. In some of our classes, notably law and psychology, we stage incidents and ask students to write what they see, and then laugh at the wide disparity of the reports. But in history we take an account of an event which has been retold many times and teach it as truth. We are undisturbed by the fact that American History is one thing south of the Mason-Dixon line, another north of it, and still another in Canada. Equally good examples can be extracted from each of our several subjects. I was raised on Longfellow, but know little of Whitman. That is doubtless because my English teachers knew or liked Longfellow better than Whitman. But others, especially among our younger generation, know Whitman better than Longfellow. They doubtless will meet life quite as well as I, in spite of the fact that in my youth, knowledge of Longfellow was an absolute.

Since all I get is a prognosis, knowledge can never be absolute. It is what I extract from a situation when my experience and purpose are brought to bear on what comes to me from my environment, and from which I make my prognosis. It is personal, and different from any other knowing. It is the only kind of knowing (mine and not yours) which will serve my purpose.

The knowing that will serve me best is that which I seek out of a welter of infinite possibilities. Rather than take what has served another, which he offers for my service, I will do better if I seek out my own. Maybe if I had sought out the poetry that I could use best, I would be long on Whitman, short on Longfellow. To "acquire and accept" what is given to me by someone else implies the acquisition and acceptance of what someone else thinks is good for me.

MUST WE DEPEND ON ABSOLUTES FOR SURETY?

Earlier, it has been mentioned that we like to believe in absolutes because they add to our sense of surety. More than that, we are accustomed to believe in them because most of us think the objects outside of us have meaning in themselves, whereas it has been shown that they only attain significance as we take account of them, and then they attain the significance which we assign to them. If we see that they have no meaning in themselves, but attain meaning in the light of each experiencing organism, then we see that they cannot be absolute.

To satisfy his need for surety, man is apt to assume that the things around him can be depended upon, and are therefore absolute. This probably comes from the fact that his prognosis of his surroundings in many instances is quite accurate. When he recognizes that what he gets from the things around him are only prognostic, and that those things therefore cannot be absolute, he pushes his absolutes further and further into the abstract world, until finally he settles for such abstractions as Truth, Free-

dom, or Justice. But all these concepts are relative and
related to a particular time and culture. From what we
know of perception and reality, and the subjective, personal nature of these phenomena, about the only depend-
able fact is that whatever tomorrow will be, it will be
different. New order is continually springing into form,
and deteriorating into disorder. Schroedinger[1] points out
that the atomic arrangements of the gene is the most per-
sistent and permanent phenomenon in nature, but it is
never the same in two individuals. When nature provides
that the new individual shall come from two others, she
provides for a sort of permanence, but also for change.

WE ARE CERTAIN OF CHANGE

If we look upon life as a flowing and becoming process,
implied from the nature of perception and reality, that
the present is a momentary springboard for more becoming, then the fact of change becomes increasingly important. It really becomes something which we can accept
as a constant. The most successful and adjusted people
then will be those who know that whatever tomorrow
may be, it must be different from today or yesterday, and
who are ready, know how, and have assurance to meet
tomorrow on that basis. They will not be filled with anxiety about tomorrow because they will have confidence
and courage with which to meet it. They are the forward-
looking people, as against the ones with eyes on the past,
clinging to some sort of material or abstract absolute.

WHAT ABOUT AUTHORITIES?

These ideas make trouble for those who would pose
as authorities. It is true that one person can know more
about some item than others. He can never know all about

[1] "What Is Life?" Erwin Schroedinger, Macmillan, 1945.

it, but he has selected one thing and has worked to improve his prognosis of it. Sometimes we say he knows more and more about less and less. But you and I can never get into his exact place, and we can never really make a fact ours completely because he says it is so. When we take it and fit it into our background, we take only the parts which we can make fit. It is then ours uniquely, and no longer his. We can of course learn from others, but we can only learn those parts of what others can offer which we can fit into *our* experience and purpose.

This makes the teacher's role as an authority untenable. In fact, he makes endless unnecessary trouble for himself in assuming this role. For what he can ever know about his subject is certain to be incomplete and tentative. If he is under the burden of making his students believe he is an authority, he has to delimit what his students can learn to what he knows. I once was a member of a class in botany, where the professor planned to take the class out to study all of the plant life in a limited area. The day before this field trip he went out and pulled up every plant in the area which he did not know.[2] This delimited our learning possibilities to what the professor knew in advance. If he had not assumed the role of an authority, we could have all learned from each other, and the professor might even have learned from some of us. We do the same thing when we insist that students confine themselves to the textbook.

An essential is something which someone in authority has decided must be learned by everybody on authority. It is an absolute good, else it would not be essential. The fact seems to be that in our becoming world, some of the essentials are bound to be missed by some people, others by others. It would thus appear that there is no item of

---

[2] Admitted later in a careless moment of camaraderie.

human knowledge that somebody could not get along without. We say that everyone must learn to read, but reading is not knowledge itself, but a tool for obtaining knowledge. It is a fine tool, and each of us will have his powers greatly enhanced by it.

While many of us have lived happy and successful lives without ever learning to read, it surely is a useful tool of which each of us should strive to get control. It will increase the possibility of our knowing, and to know is to add further to our powers. Even after we have learned to read, we are confronted with such a mass of miscellaneous reading material that we can never get much of it, and no two of us can get the same. There are certain big masses of information which we would probably be unable to miss, but not one of these would necessarily make or break us.

SUBJECT MATTER ALONE CANNOT EDUCATE

Subject matter set out to be learned can be learned to a degree. It can be briefly stored against examination day, but unless it attains more meaning than the requirements of that day—unless its meaning takes on importance to the learning person—it will not abide long. In fact, it might be said not to have been learned at all, but perhaps only memorized, since when we learn, a modification of the organism is said to occur. That is, the organism behaves differently after true learning has taken place.

Certainly the acquiring of such subject matter cannot be said to be educational in itself. We all know people who have acquired much subject matter and have remained uneducated. We use the contradictory term "educated fools" in describing them. Something more than superficial acquisition seems to be necessary to make knowledge function, and to produce the educated man.

This integration, being individual and personal, cannot be coerced, even by the person doing the learning. He cannot even coerce himself. This will be a great blow to many teachers, because they have proceeded on the theory that if they kept Johnny in after school and *made* him learn one of the teacher's absolutes, he would become educated.

THE FRAGMENTATION OF KNOWLEDGE

Perception and its resulting reality is definitely related to wholes. We extract meaning from our surroundings as a whole. This meaning is as broad as life itself. It cannot be felt or understood in segments. So accustomed are we to comprehending wholes that we seem to have little power to put separate pieces together. If we want to get a better prognosis of a particular item in our surroundings, we may try to single it out, briefly and to a degree, but never entirely, except in schools or laboratories. As I walk to the office, I call upon science, language, mathematics, history, geography, and the rest all together. Especially is this true if I have to solve any special problem in the act. It would seem then that these special bits of knowledge ought not to be separated out by themselves in school but situations should be approached as wholes, with all the elements involved. Thus would mathematics, for example, become a living reality in use, rather than an abstraction for which the learner sees little use. It might be difficult thus to teach twelve-year-olds to invert the divisor and multiply in order to divide one fraction by another. But then maybe a twelve-year-old does not need to know how to divide one fraction by another. Even if he might need it sometime, there seems doubt that he can truly learn it, and so should not have his living clouded by it.

If we want to produce whole men, we will have to abandon our efforts to train or educate them in parts. We will have to stop doing things to him to train his memory, his will power, his reasoning power, etc. When a man meets a problem in his becoming world, he meets it with all he has—foot, ear, fist, purpose, value. These have to be marshalled together to meet not some, but all phases of the problem. Psychologists have long known this, but we teach just as though it had never been discovered. Some psychologists even teach that fact by a method which belies their belief in it.

CHILDREN SHOULD EXPERIENCE ALL KINDS OF PEOPLE

In school, we fragmentize our child society much as we do what we set out to be learned. Whereas in life whole men meet and cope with all kinds of people, children really meet only those who are their own age, often to the half year, and frequently are further placed only with children of the same ability in dealing with abstractions. Not uncommonly they are placed only with those of their own sex. The perceptions possible under such isolated circumstances are bound to give an incomplete picture of life as it must be lived. Selections are artificially made in advance.

This is perhaps logical if we believe, as we seem to, that education is a solitary, not a social process. What we have learned of perception and its personal nature should most certainly result in the rejection of this idea. If the school is to be unsocial, and we cannot educate each one in a solitary cubicle, then the next best we can do is to place the child with people who are as nearly like himself as possible. We aim at the most obvious similarities, age, sex, and ability according to our measuring scales.

But man is a social being, either by nature or by force

of circumstance, and his problem of adjustment is with other people even more than with things. It is difficult for him to get communion with another being as discussed in Chapter IV, which he must have to a degree if he is to be truly social. No item of surroundings, thing or fact, can ever be the same to teacher as to learner, or to two different learners, no matter how much we group them on the basis of similarities. So it would appear that to educate a child he should be thrown with as many different kinds of people as possible. He should meet them as whole people, faced with concrete problems. The social needs of man and the difficulty of communion would demand that learners help one another, and that solutions should be reached by the best means available, not the hard way. The cooperative way of life, calling for mutual help and appreciation of different points of view, cannot be achieved in isolation.

SCHOOL AS PREPARATION

Since life is a becoming process, ever novel and ever personal, preparation for life (as our schools would do it) becomes impossible. We cannot store up a whole situation. It is true that the adult, in meeting a novel situation, uses his past experience. He will be prepared for it by the degree to which he can be given experiences which bear upon it. If a child in school can be given a rich variety of experiences, close to the concrete, he may have the experiential background needed to cope with any given situation. This differs from attempting to store fragments of knowledge against later need, because fragments of knowledge, given as absolutes, never come into experiential consciousness. If they are in fact successfully stored at all, they lack the practicality of the concrete experience.

Instead of teaching a child of six to read because he will

sometime need to read, we might let the need for reading come out of what he is doing. Rather than teach him arithmetic, as a thing apart, he could be allowed to develop its need. In fact, instead of dealing primarily with abstractions—letters, numbers, and the like (as we now do)—he might learn his abstractions in relation to and after the concretions from which they arise. In this case, the number of abstractions with which he would deal would be greatly reduced in number and increased in meaning.

CHILDREN HAVE THEIR OWN PURPOSES

In Chapter III we gave great emphasis to the importance of valueful purpose. The purpose of the individual, which may be influenced by the codescript of the gene, is essential to the process of extracting meaning out of surroundings through perception. When we receive a stimulus pattern, we depend to a degree upon our past experience as to which of an infinity of coincidences or externalities we choose to attend to. But past experience is not enough to account for the fine selection of these coincidences which we make. If we had only our experience to guide us, we would have to pay attention to all the coincidences which came within our experience. We do not do this; we select only that part of the scene which has something to do with our purposes. So the meaning extracted from the scene is not only unique to the viewing person on account of this individual experiential background, but also because of unique purpose. This makes a perception doubly personal and subjective.

Perhaps there is no common practice in school that is so damaging, then, as our violation of the learner's purpose. Since we believe now that his purpose is really part of the machinery involved in perception, it becomes wellnigh impossible for him even to have experiences on the strength of purposes other than his own. So when we make children "learn" that for which they see no need, it is doubtful that learning goes on at all. Certain it is that he learns vastly more about teachers as people than he does about the abused subject matter. I use the word "abused" here because what the teacher sought to have learned probably has value, but here it becomes a sort of battleground or bone of contention, a pawn between two conflicting sets of purposes. Any bit of human knowledge, even the ablative absolute, deserves better treatment.

RESPONSIBILITY, CITIZENSHIP, DISCIPLINE

If we teach in accordance with the student's purpose (and what we know about perception would seem to demand it) then we can only teach what the student can purpose to learn. Thus we have to abandon the "essentials." If we teach in accordance with the student's purpose to learn, then the problem of getting the young to assume responsibility arises. Whenever he does anything in response to his purpose, he has assumed responsibility, for it was *his* purpose, not the teacher's. When he does something in response to the purpose of another, he has not assumed responsibility, but he has obeyed orders. If the teacher is going to furnish the purpose, he must also assume the responsibility.

The good citizen must want to be a good citizen, or he will not be one. In order to do this he has to be able to see the good of his group, which he can only see to the extent that he has a chance to cooperate with his group and get experience in sharing the purposes of his group. Good citizens are well-disciplined, but if the discipline is going to be worthwhile it has to relate to his larger good as he adjusts, giving some but not all to the good of his associates. The discipline thus achieved is intrinsic to the life he is leading, rather than being imposed from above. It will not desert him when he is on his own.

We all know what happens when the young get away from long-imposed discipline. It is dangerous to be near the doorway when such a class is dismissed. If the children had been using their own purposes for what they were doing, they would not have been under imposed restriction, and would not have built up a "head of steam." Our society needs people who have had experience in *self*-control while they are young, so that they will have practice in exercising it when they are free from the teacher or parent.

REWARDS AND PUNISHMENT AS COERCION

To get children to pursue our purposes we have invented a most elaborate system of rewards and punishments. These are all extrinsic, that is, they lie outside the task itself. We give Junior a nickel if he will eat his cereal, although there is no connection between nickel and cereal. Later we give him "A" if he works hard and successfully on his geometry, but the reward lies outside the geometry. When one works in response to his own purposes, the reward for success or the punishment for failure lies in the act itself, and in the good he had hoped to achieve. If a book is read, it should be read because finding out what is in the book brings satisfaction to the reader or has significance in use, not so he can report on a number of pages to the teacher.

In connection with purpose, the question of coercion arises. Coercion implies the inflicting of the will of one upon another. It can never bring about the best kind of learning. It is certain to be accompanied by many adverse associated learnings. The child may learn that the teacher is an undesirable person, for example. He may find that there are many ways to beat the game. It may be necessary to use coercion on rare occasions, more or less of an emergency nature, but we should know what we are doing when we use it, recognize that its uses are limited and that it is accompanied by many undesirable side learnings. The learner will still make his own selections from the current situation, and they are likely to be different from the ones desired by the coercing adult.

THE VALUE OF MISTAKES

In true problem solving, the problem must be real, that is, it must be so contrived that its solution becomes important to the learner. It is the task of the teacher to contrive learning experiences, but not to coerce outcomes. The teacher who pretends not to control outcomes but does so, is more harmful than the overt autocrat, because children can learn more easily how to combat the autocrat. When a teacher contrives an experience, he must be willing to accept the fact that each student will get something different out of it, and that some will not profit by it at all.

The learning experience must provide for trial and error, with a recognition of the fact that more is often learned by what we do wrong than by what we do right. We miseducate almost universally in that we fail to realize the educative value of mistakes. We follow our children around to see to it that they do not do anything wrong. This does not take account of the fact that doing things wrong, with its attendant frustration, is the very essence of growth. Without error there is no call for contriving. If the problem is unreal, as in the ordinary arithmetic class, its answer becomes entirely unimportant. In any problem, real or unreal, it is the contriving, the cut-

and-try, the failure followed by success, which adds to the experiential background of the learner.

Evaluation constitutes a large part of our day at school. There is of course nothing wrong with evaluation in itself. It is part of the very flow of life. Every time we make a choice we make an evaluation. Even when we select what we will attend to in the perception we entertain, we are evaluating. But note that it is *our* evaluation, not one made by someone else. The purposing, contriving learner should make his own evaluations, reflected in the satisfaction of the purposes which he feels. What I do may be evaluated by my colleagues as it affects them, and my social or unsocial conduct may be reflected in their attitudes toward me. But this is different (more intrinsic) than evaluation as it is used in schools, where it is the basis for extrinsic reward or punishment and is part of the whole scheme of coercion, or getting learners to operate on purposes other than their own.

This is not to imply that the teacher should not make any evaluation of students at all, although his evaluation of his own procedures should be fully as fruitful. It means that much less of the teacher's and student's time should be thus spent. More time could then be spent on learning something to evaluate. The teacher's evaluations of students should test growth rather than the student's ability to give back abstractions; and they should be designed to help the student in his own realistic evaluation and to show how teacher and student together can bring their resources to bear on growth. The teacher should make use of new devices for ascertaining the student's degree of surety and his ability to contrive new responses in the face of failure and frustration. There would be no place for the altogether too common punitive motive in evaluation.

Learning must start with concretions—with what we may call the "how-to-do." It is in this world of action, since perceptions are directives for action, that new experiences are accumulated. Certain abstractions will be useful tools, and will naturally arise. Operating in this moving world of "how-to-do," the learner will be confronted with natural problems which he must solve. As he contrives he will do many things that will not work. This will call for re-evaluating what has been done, and new trials. The attempt, the evaluation, the success, all play their part in taking a person from inadequacy to adequacy. The whole process is growth in its widest meaning; growth which enables the whole organism to become more competent to cope with life.

CHAPTER VI

Education Can Be More Real

Many are the ills of the world as we stumble forward in suspicion and fear, toward what may well be our doom. And much of the responsibility must be laid to our schools, which represent our sole over-all effort to produce adequate people. Many parents and teachers wonder at the portion dealt our young in what we call education, and wish that the process could somehow become a more meaningful, pleasant, and satisfying experience.

Again referring to the demonstrations at The Hanover Institute and what they show with regard to the nature of perception and reality, it would seem, if we may oversimplify, that many of the ills of our education and of our educational product (our people) come from two major errors: (1) That we present knowledge as absolute and existing before learning can begin, instead of something to be lived; and (2) that we disregard and often work counter to the learner's purpose, *in the light of which his very perceptions arise.* Most of the other ills, such as extrinsic motivation and coercion, come from these.

We do not *have* to continue to waste our educational strength going counter to the powerful tide of the learner's purpose. We do not always *have* to paddle upstream. We can start to work *with* the observable forces instead of *against* them. Parents who desire a better life

73

for their children, and who cry out against their children's chains, can secure it.

I shall next attempt to describe in part what such a school might be like. I make no defense of the particular items here set forth. Another person would use different particulars. The basic criterion in choosing educational procedures is that they must be in keeping with what we now know to be the basis of perception and the nature of reality. They must conform to the fact that perception is the product of unique past experience and unique value purposes.

Nor should anyone think that a transition from the kind of schooling we now know to the kind here described could be quickly and easily attained. We are all products of the traditional school, and its habits are deeply imbedded, even in those of us who have come to doubt the value of the procedures which were used upon us. We would need to go forward with caution, learning ourselves as we go, trying techniques which may fail in part, and starting anew. We would have to train ourselves not to be on the defensive over any procedure simply because it is ours. The trial and error recommended for students would be equally imperative for teachers. But with an open mind and a clear notion of how perceptions can be acquired by the learner, certain types of activities would be indicated while others would obviously be unsuited.

The description can never be in more than general terms, because what we do next Monday morning at nine o'clock can never be decided without consideration of the children and teachers who are going to do it. However, general lines can be indicated and concrete illustrations can be given to sharpen the generalities. But real concretions only exist with individuals. They depend upon who you are and what you are dealing with. We become concrete when the person acts on his present perception.

In case there are those among us who love their money more than their young, it is only fair to say that the school here discussed will not be a cheap school. The general notion that education can be done cheaply completely fails to take into account the extremely complex nature of a child's development. The teachers will have to have no more children in their classes than they can properly teach. This is a sound economic policy—no manufacturer would consider it good business to give a worker twice the amount of work that he could do. Yet we do this in schools. To illustrate, if we can say that a teacher can teach twenty-five pupils but cannot teach fifty, we often give her fifty and believe that we have saved the salary of a teacher. We have not in fact saved the salary of a teacher, but have lost a teacher. Teachers will have to be well enough paid so that they can devote their time to their teaching, without worry and without having to peddle something in their spare time. And considering the value involved, the cost will not be more than the American people can afford once they see where their treasure lies. We use our money for what we value most. We buy what we want. The cost of adequate education will probably not exceed what we now spend for alcoholic beverages, a tax which we do not seem to mind too much.

It *will* mean doubling and perhaps trebling what is now spent for education.

THE GENERAL SCOPE

The school should start with what we now call preschool or nursery school. It is then that experiences are being laid down upon which the child must build the rest of his knowledge. The early years are of utmost importance. When children develop unsocial attitudes and habits of thought during the first six years of their lives, any school which they might attend is at a great disadvantage. Children can and should start to learn social living very young, and education is above all else a social enterprise. Besides, in keeping with the principle that children should mingle with others of all ages, it would be good for the older children to have very young ones in the same building with them. They could learn child care by this contact; in fact, a great deal of the care of the very young could be assumed by the older children.

What we know as grade levels would not be recognized. Taking the example of helping with child care, eight-year-olds and twelve-year-olds could and would be working side by side. Of course there would be some tendency for children in like stages of development to work at similar levels. When children come together in this way, it is in keeping with their purposes, not their ages or I.Q.'s, and is in no way damaging; in fact it is likely to be profitable. It is the artificial grouping of children for adult convenience and for isolation which is to be avoided. This was doubtless one of the great advantages of the one-room country school. It had all ages and kinds of children within one room, and while the teacher labored hard to create the artificiality of grade levels, she never quite succeeded, and children of differing ages, sexes, and abilities were forced to deal with each other. We often hear the virtues of the little red school house extolled by the nostalgic, and indeed it seemed to do pretty well. Perhaps this was the reason. Certainly it could not have been due to teacher-training, or to building and equipment.

In many schools today it is necessary to dismiss the

younger children early because the older ones will abuse them if they are not safe at home before general dismissal. This is as sad a commentary as one could find on the unsocial results coming from isolation and unfamiliarity with children of other ages. This is segregation in full flower.

There would be no promotions, no time when everybody moves up a notch all at once, any more than there is in life. When a child finishes a task or project, he moves on to another, but this is no more a promotion than it is when one stops rolling a ball and starts hitting it with a bat. It is a matter of individual growth; it goes on continuously and the changes are gradual.

The school would operate the year around, and for this reason, among others, promotion time would not be necessary. There would never be what we now know as a "term" of school, with everyone being turned loose at once. The ossification of institutions is nowhere better displayed than in our summer vacation. It comes from the time when children were needed to tend and harvest crops. It is quite out of place now except in rural areas. Children are thrown upon their own resources with nothing to do for a period of from ten to sixteen weeks. If they have acquired any of the "set-out-to-be-learned" knowledge, they lose most of it through disuse during this time. Too often the only lasting feature of the past year's work is the mark on the records in the principal's office.

The teachers in the old days usually lived in the community and had other means of support. Now they are thrown out of work for a period each year, and must clerk in stores, work in factories, or do whatever else they can find in order to live. This work in the world outside of school has value for teachers as experience, but should not be an economic necessity. Teachers ought to be able to take a year off occasionally in order to keep in touch with the outside world.

Children and teachers alike should of course have vacations, but they should not all come at once, and the vacation should be an individual matter, just as it is in most other types of employment. If a child, his parents, and his teachers think he should take the month of January, for example, for a vacation, there is no reason why he should not do so, and the school would run on just the same. Growth would not stop during vacation; it would constitute a different kind of educative experience. Since he would be working on *his* projects, he could pick them up or let them drop when he got back. The period of growth during his vacation might make the project meaningless on his return. He would not have missed a certain number of pages which we think have to be made up but never really can be. The emergence of a concrete situation in a creative enterprise can never be recaptured. Our usual make-up is merely "covering the ground" and is often punitive, to deter absence.

The child would continue to attend the school until he became ready to do something else. This would be until he went into employment or into higher education. This could come any time he was ready. His readiness for employment would be greatly enhanced by the work-study program, which will be briefly described later. In times of plentiful employment, if we are ever to have such except in war, he would leave school at a younger age than in times of scarce employment. Young people also vary greatly in the age at which they are ready to go to college. They should go when they are ready. This readiness implies emotional as much as intellectual maturity. Transferring students to college before the usual graduation from high school is not new. The University of Chicago has done it for some time. During the war, when college students were scarce, a number of universities experimented with the idea. It is not known whether the welfare of the student was the first consideration at that time, but the students seem to have done very well.

Thus there would be no graduation—no wholesale exodus, willy-nilly, whether people are ready to leave or not. The graduation spectacle is one of the oddest in American life. On a certain day we tell approximately one-fourth of our high-school population that we no longer have anything to offer them. Some of them would have been able to leave a long time before, and many are not yet ready. It is as though we made them all jump off a springboard at once, with only a few knowing how to swim. It would seem sensible not to give up one activity until the next one had been planned, and planning should be an important part of school experience.

Part of the education of urban children should take place in rural settings. City life is very artificial. Milk comes in bottles. Pieces of paper are the medium of exchange. There are many possibilities for education in a large city, but man grievously needs to have a chance to make contact somewhere with the good earth from which he sprang. He cannot forever deny this heritage. In the country, life springs up all around. The mysteries of the earth itself, of plant and animal husbandry, of procreation and of decay, teach the lessons of life as no city pavement can do.

With our habit of summer vacation, some try to achieve this through summer camps. Only the most economically fortunate are able to afford this, except a very few who are so poor that they get into charity camps. The great bulk of children never get this opportunity. The summer is not the only time that the earth is educative; she has varying lessons to teach at all times of year. And most summer camps, operated as private enterprise, are not really educative. They are a cross between mass recreation and mass regimentation. They often do the parents who stay at home more good than they do the children.

THE BUILDINGS

It goes without saying that the urban buildings would have the best and latest in construction, just as many of our newer schools have now. Much is now known about lighting, for instance, which is essential to a good healthful environment. We have ruined the eyes of untold numbers of children by requiring them to read books in musty old buildings without proper light. This is an unnecessary destruction of a great asset, especially since vision is so important to our perception. New discoveries in heating and ventilation would also add to the comfort and efficiency of children.

Buildings should be simple in architecture, with the emphasis on use. They should be so constructed that they open out to the world around them, rather than turning those in them away from the world. Being light and airy, they would be free from the familiar institutional odors so common to our schools today.

To the extent that it is possible, they should be built so that they could be changed to give maximum use under changing needs and conditions. Many of the partitions could be built so that they could be taken out or moved, giving different sized rooms from time to time. The rooms should be accessible to each other without going into the halls. This adds to the possibility for doing things together. With the emphasis on use, the furniture must all be usable by the children who work there. Every piece of furniture, so far as possible, should be movable and adaptable to the size of the children. The simple expedient of soundproofing can increase freedom to make noise.

There should be many places for children to do things. This calls for laboratories, gymnasiums, stage sets, all kinds of arts, music, wood, and metal shops, photography equipment, and the like. There would be many books in each room, so that the children could have ready access to them when they want them. The children would have a hand in choosing the books in the light of ongoing activities. In addition, a central library would be necessary. But it would not be a forbidding place such as many of our libraries now are, designed to keep children from using books, and founded on the principle that every child is a potential book thief. Children should have ready access to the books, and should learn early how to find what they want. Books then would not be stolen or mutilated, but would be worn out. When a child mutilates a book he usually does so to get even with some adult. He has the regrettable habit of classing all adults together, and he does not necessarily mutilate the book belonging to the adult who has thwarted him.

The grounds of the urban school should be used for play and for growing what may be grown there. They should have beauty, but a varying beauty put there by each succeding set of young people. They should have beautiful lawns made by the children, but the grass should never be held in higher esteem than the child. The school grounds should always be seen as a means or device for educating.

The buildings in the rural setting should be even more temporary and movable than those of the urban. These could be built and rebuilt by succeeding generations of children, built for use by those who build them.

Depending upon the amount of space to be had, many kinds of sports should be available. The opportunity to learn to play all the usual games—learning with others of about the same ability—should be available. Different tastes an abilities should be taken into account in sports, as in all other activities. The possibilities in sports and games for learning cooperative living should be continuously exploited.

It is customary now to tell a hundred children that at ten o'clock they are ready to play, and are ready to play the same game. Usually the game is one at which only a few excel, and the others never get a real chance to learn, even if they wanted to, which they do not. Not infrequently they develop an aversion to sport from this unsatisfactory experience which lasts throughout life. Either a game is for fun or it is for some other purpose. If it is for fun, it should be played at a time and in a way that can be enjoyed. Fun should not be regarded as frivolous, but a real living and learning experience.

THE CURRICULUM

What would go on in a school which operated on the basis that the child's sense of reality comes from his unique perception and has to be developed alongside of other individuals with whom he can have no common world? The specific answers cannot be found in a book such as this, because it is too far removed from the concretions with which children must deal. Any specific blueprint would be certain to fail, in part at least, when the persons involved put their own needs into the picture. Many of our schools seem to be ineffective because we get the building, the materials, the curriculum, and the teachers all ready, and then the wrong student body comes to school. Any curriculum set up in advance is bound to fail, because education is an emerging process.

Certain it is that we should provide completely for the physical health of the children. This not only involves activities that will enlighten them about the structure and function of their bodies, but also thorough physical examinations and correction of defects. No child need go through school and life starved or thwarted because the simple facts of correction and nutrition are ignored. In our present schools we often do not bother to determine simple physical ailments, perhaps because we fancy that our task is to feed the mind separate from the body. When we do learn of physical defects we may tell the parents about them but the parents do as they please about their correction. No parent has the right to deny correction of handicapping physical defects to his children. We do not allow a parent to decide what shall be done about smallpox, yet he may decide to let his child get along with glandular imbalance, poor sight, or decayed teeth.

In the same manner, the mental health of the child must be our concern. Many of the ills of the mind arise out of school. The thwarting which brings this about can be avoided. Further, most mental ills, like the physical, are possible of improvement and cure through proper treatment. We are coming to realize more and more that there is no place where we can draw the line between physical and mental illness, since we see the organism as a whole and recognize that the body does for us pretty much what we want it to do. Close attention to mental health, and treatment where needed, are essential in the modern school. There must be no frustration for its own sake, nor must the child experience frustration beyond his ability to cope with it. Attention to mental health implies psychiatric treatment when needed, just as we would set broken bones. When children are pursuing their own purposes, extrinsic frustration will be so eliminated that the need for treatment in mental health will be greatly reduced.

The activities of the day would involve much doing. Education would start with concrete activity, and useful abstractions would come out of it. The opportunities to do and to explore would be infinite. These explorations would pose problems to be solved, with freedom to make mistakes, to cut and try, to fail and to contrive. There would be emphasis on doing those things for which the doer has use, not just in aimless activity for activity's sake. To be sure, doings that might seem aimless or profitless in an adult's eyes do not necessarily seem so to the child, and the activity must be on the level to which the child has developed. For example, a child might want to make a little sailboat. To us, it might seem only play, because we know he will never be able to sail in it. But to him it can be of almost deadly importance. Incidentally, older children might very well devote time to making a boat that will float and carry them. It would involve concrete action, wherein objects take on reality; it would call for use of abstractions—mathematics, books on boat building, and the like—and it would attain full validity through use. But this illustration becomes valueless if the children under consideration care nothing about boats, but happen to be concerned about something else. Whenever an activity serves the purpose of taking a person where he is and promoting his growth toward competency and adequacy that activity becomes educative.

Thus the concrete actions indulged in would be in keeping with what the learner purposes. Since we know that the very selections from his surroundings which he is able to see depend upon his purpose, we cannot proceed otherwise whether we like it or not. This does not mean that the teacher has no right to try to develop interest. What the teacher has no right to do is to attempt to demand interest. She must be interested herself, and the child then lends interest because there is rapport. Children can be stimulated to wholesome and useful activity, but it has to become *their* activity. We sometimes argue that children like to be told what to do. This is often true, because we all like to avoid responsibility, and we get surety from letting the teacher or someone else take the responsibility. But we do not really grow in this way. We only grow when we face life and get our surety from our own contrived actions.

The activities undertaken would be with many kinds of children, according to similar purposing. Thus a fourteen-year-old and a nine-year-old might well be working on the same project. In that case the older would often be teacher to the younger. For most undertakings we need different kinds of people. The smaller child can often do parts of the enterprise which the older cannot do, or can do only with great difficulty.

There would be no fragmentation of knowledge, but the teachers would be ever ready to help get the whole set of implications out of each novel and developing situation.[1] Reading and ciphering would come out of the need to be able to do more interesting and complex things. History would abandon the chronological approach, where we teach the child first what is furthest from him, and never do quite catch up to the present or make the

[1] A fuller description of this type of education can be found in Mac-Connell, Melby, and Arndt's "New School For a New Culture," Harper & Brothers, 1943.

events come alive with significance for what is now going on.

Since the details of the curriculum are to be derived from the learner, planning would be an essential part of the day's work. Children, having identified a problem, would plan with each other and with the teacher. Planning what you are going to do is essential if you are to follow your own purposes. If you are going to pursue the purposes of another, you do not need to plan. Planning is the tentative layout of the assault on a problem. It is often painful and time-consuming, but plainly essential. It is almost universally omitted when knowledge is set out to be learned. Teachers now say that planning takes too long, and so they omit an essential in the process of learning, that of cutting out what is to be done.

Probably there is no teacher who would not say that education should aid the student in problem solving. Problem solving, along with critical thinking, has become an educational cliché. But so far as the student is concerned, the first part of the process is almost universally omitted. The sizing up of the situation, the decision as to whether the problem is worth attack, and which way to go about it—these are all done for the student in advance. Only the less educational part of the problem remains; the carrying out of the plan, which is bound to work because the teacher has done it many times before, is of very little value. This seems even clearer now that we know that the teacher and the student cannot even see the same problem, much less contrive the same way in its solution.

Planning can of course be done alone, but it usually involves other people, and always does when a group enterprise is undertaken. The process of getting group agreement on what is to be done, deciding who will do the separate parts, and what the first attack shall be, is the essence of cooperation. It is a group experience children must have if they are to learn to work together outside of school. Here is where cooperation and group solidarity is taught even better than in the execution of the plan, for here one must learn to give and take, to submerge a little for his own greater good, to give part of his desire in order to have help on the rest. He thus helps himself best. The value of help is here best expressed, for he learns that if he shares another's burdens, and the other shares his, both become lighter, and more achievement becomes possible.

Particularly is planning and participation called for in the area of school government. Children enjoy an orderly society if it is *their* order, and rules which we ourselves invent and which we feel promote our good do not become something for us to break. Learning how to govern, like everything else, comes from having experience in governing. True leadership can only emerge where all have a chance to become leaders. Each individual will thus gain experience in following—each will be both leader and follower. The failure of our present educational methods is nowhere better shown than in the very low degree of capacity our citizens have for participating intelligently in their government. This is most inexcusable because a school is a society in miniature, with nearly all of the problems of the larger society. It is an unused laboratory in responsible citizenship.

As soon as students are old enough, their school experience should be supplemented by work experience in the actual working world. Our youth do not need to come to maturity without having the slightest idea what the working world is like. They can hold part-time jobs, and work in teams. The amount of time that they should spend in outside work would vary with different students, and no two need to do it exactly alike. Some of the school time at this stage should be spent in discussion and evaluation of the work experience. This discussion and evaluation is what makes the difference between plain work and work as an educational device.

Cooperation of the community, both employer and labor, would be needed for the successful operation of the work-study program. This would become the school's best opportunity to be an integral part of the community. The separation of school and community now so common and so damaging could thus in part be dispelled. The employer would then come to see himself as educator, and the doings of the school would be of interest to him. He now fancies the school a place to stay away from, populated with strange people whom he does not understand. It seems an excellent place to cut taxes. But if he himself is involved as educator, if the whole community sees its role and responsibility for the education of the young, its activities will not be curtailed or reduced.

Workers would of course resist giving employment to young people if they saw it as a threat or as competition. But labor has always been generous in support of education once it saw what was needed and involved. It would readily see that a small fraction of the work of the world belongs to youth as education. Labor would get the same interest derived from sharing in the enterprise that would come to the employer.

Guidance would become an important function, dealing with all children, not just the ones already in trouble. Most of the guidance would be done by the teachers and would be an integral part of the curriculum. Every child would be known well by many teachers. It has often been said that no child ever became delinquent who had one real adult friend who actually cared what became of him. Special guidance officials might be necessary, especially in the work-study program. The spectacle of assigning a child to a curriculum which he follows for four years would be untenable in the light of what we know about how children learn and grow.

Most of the maintenance work of the school would be done by the children. The tasks would be welcomed by them because they would be self-imposed. There would, of course, be need for a person in charge, to assure continuity. This person, known in our schools as the janitor, would be one of the chief educational forces of the school. Instead of being looked down upon as a menial, as is so often the case now, he would be regarded as a regular member of the teaching force. It often seems that the only persons in our schools today who deal with the concrete are the janitors.

Everything done by the child would be done in recognition of the fact that, since perception is only a prognosis and never right, he must be wrong, at least to a degree. Knowing we must be wrong enables us to work toward better prognoses and better results. The person who feels that he must be right, when he never is, works under a great handicap. For our prognostic perceptions are directives for action, and because they are only prognostic, our actions often fail. The person who feels he must be right gets such emotional reaction from this faulty performance that he is blinded to the lessons to be derived from it. He is therefore handicapped in contriving new responses. He cannot enjoy the failure and success, the cut-and-try, which is the essence of problem solving. When he learns to approach failure without emotion, he is ready for more contriving, and thus there needs to be no ultimate failure.

Children should learn to enjoy and appreciate the fact that what they do may turn out wrong and have to be revised. That is the real spirit of adventure which flavors life. To be always right, if it were possible, would be deadly dull, and one would never learn anything. We only learn when our set of responses fails to take us where we want to go. Instead of following our children around to keep them from making mistakes, we should help them learn that making a faulty try is not a sin. It is the way, and the only way, that new doors open to growth. If a child gets the idea that to make a mistake is to sin, so great is his fear of error that he refuses to try, and retires into inaction. His capacity to act becomes inhibited, and he loses contact with the reality to be gained through action. The only sin involved is on the part of the adult who deprives youth of freedom to make mistakes.[2]

EVALUATION

The most important evaluation in such a school would be precisely the one made by the student himself, who undertakes, experiences faulty action, and contrives better. If we wish to test him, we can test him in areas that really matter, and indeed we should do so in order that we may contribute more to his growth. We could test him on his sense of surety when we confront him with

[2] In an article by Paul de Kruif in *The Reader's Digest*, November, 1945, "Boss Kettering, The Man Who Fails Forward," Mr. C. F. Kettering is quoted as saying, "If only there were a million more boys being taught what it takes to be a researcher, what a world this could be! Think of the poor kids, from the time they start to school, they're examined three or four times a year, and if they flunk, it's a disgrace. If they fail once, they're out. In contrast, all research is 99.9 percent failure and if you succeed once, you're in. Here's what we ought to teach them: The only time you don't want an experiment to fail is the last time you try it."

conflicting clues. We could study his reaction in the distorted room (see Chapter III) when he learns his action has been faulty. We could study his response to frustration, as to whether it strengthens or weakens his determination. These would test a child in matters which really make a difference as he goes forth to cope with the world. How much more useful this information would be than the knowledge we gain about a child from his memory feats involving abstractions!

Surely we would not submit to the folly of abandoning the present objectives of education and then measuring our product by their yardsticks. We would not submit the student to the same examinations given by schools with other objectives. When he finishes school he would surely know more than the usual high school graduate, but it would be a different kind of knowledge, and, I believe, a more useful one.

If we mentioned his "intelligence" at all (a dubious practice) it would be in terms of his capacity to contrive new responses to novel situations rather than ability based on facility in language or mathematics.

This is one of the places where our past experimentation in education has fallen down. There are many among us who have been dissatisfied with the "set-out-to-be-learned" type of education, and who have tried many ways of modifying present educational practice. There is nothing proposed in this chapter which has not been tried and done successfully. But I feel that too often these experimenters have permitted themselves to be judged by the old criteria. Too often they have said they could accomplish the same ends as the traditional school, in a better way. Yet if we change our approach and our procedures, we must also change our expected outcomes.

It would be folly to claim that the children who go through a school as here described would be as well versed in all the abstractions—which some think constitute human knowledge—as the ones who had done nothing else. I believe that they would be more competent to meet life, more inventive, more creative, more adequate. The only evaluation which really matters in education is how the educated meets life, what his capacities for adjustment are, and what quality of life he is able to achieve. The answer will be found in life as it is lived.

The salient points of the school then would be: (1) we would try to ride with rather than against the tide of purpose; (2) we would start with children at a much younger age; (3) we would start with the concrete and let needed abstractions come from them; (4) we would keep knowledge in wholes; (5) we would work to develop a sense of surety; (6) we would use the community as an educational force and device; (7) we would use both rural and urban settings; (8) we would emphasize planning and cooperation as essential parts of personal or group problem solving; (9) we would cherish the value of failure and contriving.

There would, of course, be objections from many quarters to this type of school. Some would not want to modify long-established habits. Some would be fearful that they would not be able to fit into a school of concrete doing. Some would think such a school would not be "hard" enough, unwilling to abandon the old idea that if a thing is hard to do it must be good to do. Some would doubtless revive the old stories which have always been invented to ridicule efforts to find new ways to educate. A few of these objections will be dealt with in the next chapter. It would not be easy, either for students or teachers, but it would not be made hard just for the sake of hardness. It would be as easy and as hard as life itself. The difficulties encountered would be only those inherent in what is to be done when problems are faced and solved. These difficulties have always seemed sufficient to me.

CHAPTER VII

The Teacher and Subject Matter

Judging by the fate of much of the educational experimentation that has gone on in the past, many objections will be raised to the kind of education just described. Some of these objections are honest queries by those who would welcome new patterns and who are seeking ways to attain them. Other objections will be merely derisive reactions by those most fearful of departure from the tried and true.

Most of this derision we have heard. No responsible educator ever advocated, for example, that children be permitted to do exactly what they please. Yet many people believe this to be the case. Some ill-advised enthusiast may have said this to a class at one time, although I doubt it. To the average citizen, this is too often what educational experimentation means.

When the control goes from the authoritarian teacher to the demands of the group, no individual achieves the right to do exactly as he pleases. For he then becomes responsible—responsible to and for the greater good of those with whom he is associated. His freedom is limited to those activities which will advance the undertakings of his group. He has had a share in planning these undertakings, and has perforce assumed a responsibility for their advancement.

To assume that when the teacher is no longer the authoritarian each is free to do whatever enters his mind is to assume that we have only to choose between autocracy and anarchy. There is another choice, which we sometimes call democracy. This implies giving up individual goods for group goods. When a person does this, he has less freedom than he had under autocracy, for when he was under the autocrat, the autocrat took all of the responsibility, and the student was in conscience free to do whatever he could get away with. In many cases this is a great deal. When he accepts membership in a group, with a group goal, he is no longer free to do whatever he can get away with. He has an obligation to his fellows, and status with his fellows is important to him, whereas status with the autocrat means nothing to him except to the extent that the autocrat is in a position to take punitive measures against him.

If I wanted freedom, in the sense of license to do as I pleased, I would take my chances with the autocrat for he can watch me only a certain amount of time, and I have no responsibility for his program, nor have I any rapport with him worth preserving.

Another cliché certain to be heard is the old story, told with much mirth, of the boy who came to school and asked, "Teacher, do I have to do what I want today?" This probably never occurred, though many think it did, and it could have. Instead of being relayed as a great joke, the teacher should have said, "Yes, Johnny, you will have to assume responsibility today, and every day, for your work, your play and your relationships with the others. You cannot get me to assume your responsibility by telling you what to do. This is *your* day, and you cannot look to others to be responsible for the use you make of it."

Because there is so much honest doubt and uncertainty

about what the teacher should be for, and what part
subject matter should play in education, it may be profitable to discuss them.

WHAT IS THE TEACHER FOR?

The teacher is, first of all, the continuous adult member
of the group. To say that he is a member of the group
implies that he has such rapport with the group that they
count him a member. As an adult he has more experience
and more functional knowledge than any other member.
He needs great skill in being a group member, otherwise
he will find himself the leader of the group, and his purposes will be inflicted on the group. He must be able to
advise, when asked, and to guide, when asked, without
causing the group to arrive at his predetermined goal. To
steer between being useless and authoritarian, so that he
can help the group attain its ends, is the great art of
teaching.

The teacher who pretends to help a group attain its goal
while jockeying his own ends is of course dishonest.
This is worse than the authoritarian imposition of the
teacher's goal, because it is less discernible and the student has less defense against it. When the autocrat lays out
the goal and the way of getting to it, the student then has
a chance to contrive escapes which are healthy. But the
nice teacher who makes him plan the teacher's way leaves
the student less free to rebel.

The teacher works at contriving experiences which
will be educative. He gives thought to what is to go on.
Not all experiences are educative, and the schoolroom
should be the place where it is possible, through the fore-
sight of the teacher, to enter into experiences which will
lead to richer living. This implies a choice of opportunities
for the student, made possible by all the educational re-

sources of the community and marshalled by the teacher. Not all can have the same experience, not all can profit from the same experience, but the schoolroom can provide types of doing which will reach all. The more timid and faithless will worry that the students will perversely indulge in miseducative experiences; and so they may, to a degree and for a time. But students are curious about the world in which they live, and they have their own group rapport to maintain. Each has the wholesome regard of his fellows at stake, which has a different meaning in the authoritarian classroom. The student gains status with his fellows by thwarting the purposes of the authoritarian teacher, and the powerful drive for status thus becomes antisocial, if we accept the goals of the teacher as educative.

There is a difference between the teacher contriving for his own ends, and contriving to provide rich possibilities of broad living experience for children. There is a difference between scheming to bring about predetermined outcomes and offering rich opportunities for choice, leading to growth.

The teacher is a "source" person. He is, in fact, the most important source available to any member of the group. He is not only a source of knowledge and where to find knowledge, but he is a source of emotional stability and security as well. In being available to the members of the group for knowledge and advice, the teacher needs to exercise his greatest restraint. The temptation to tell too much, and thus spoil the problem, is very strong. This can be carried to the point where the teacher becomes the end-determiner just through sheer weight of information. The teacher should give as much help as is needed for the group to get over its present dilemma, and no more.

The teacher plays a peculiar role as the adult in the life

of the child. He is often the only adult to which the child can look for security, and the importance of this role cannot be overstated. The rapport which the child establishes with the teacher is his anchor. There are some who assume that this role is filled by the parent, but this is rarely the case. There are many reasons why the parent has great difficulty in filling this role for his own child. For one thing, there is too much emotion tied up in the situation. The personal relationship between the teacher and the student, and the security which comes from it, far transcends in importance any factual knowledge which may be transmitted.

The teacher, then, is a member of the group. The moment his purpose becomes set against the purposes of the students his position becomes untenable educatively. He is the one who marshalls resources so that problems worth solving and reasonably able to be solved can be encountered. He is a source of information and technique, using his experience and knowledge to keep the problem solving going forward. He is the child's tie to the adult world, made strong by rapport and understanding. Such teaching is not easy. It calls for infinite resourcefulness. The idea that the teacher who gets students to work on their own purposes abrogates his responsibility is far from true. This kind of teaching is so difficult that it cannot be done with the number of students now commonly met by teachers in a day. That is one of the reasons why expenditures for education will have to be greatly increased. We must not ask a teacher to teach more students than he can.

WHAT IS SUBJECT MATTER FOR?

In the traditional classroom, there are really two important factors—the teacher and the subject matter. The student gets his purposes from the teacher, and he learns, if he learns, that subject matter which the teacher sets before him to learn. The subject matter remains constant, and such modification as takes place in order to bring student and subject matter together takes place in the student. If the student can find suitable goals for himself within the framework of the subject matter, well and good, but if he cannot, then he must be coerced.

Since we now know that the student learns in accordance with his own purposes and experiences, which he cannot in fact truly perceive in any other way, we must necessarily look to a modification of the role and usefulness of the subject matter. We now know that the subject matter will be perceived as the student can perceive it, no matter what we do, and that no two students will perceive a given fact the same way.

This does not mean that subject matter will not be used, or that it becomes unimportant. We cannot teach without teaching something, our students cannot learn without learning something. No piece of subject matter, no fact of human knowledge, is bad in itself. Neither is any fact good in itself. It is good or bad only in relation to the person learning it, and to the possibility of his learning it. The question becomes one of asking who the subject matter is for, whether or not he has the purpose and experience to acquire it, what its acquisition will do to and for the learner, and why it should be learned.

A stimulating experience for any teacher is to stop and ask himself why he teaches his subject. What is it for? What difference does he expect to result in his learners from having acquired it? How does it contribute to the growth of the learner? Many teachers confronted with this problem will say they teach it because it is good. This leads to the query, "Good for what? for whom? when? and why?"

While there is no parcel or fragment of human knowledge that is bad in itself, neither is there any item without which some person could not get along. It is true that there are some facts so prominent that no one who sought learning could miss them, but if he did miss them, he probably would be able to live successfully without them. Those who worry about the "minimum essentials" have some goods of their own which they feel must serve everyone, since these goods have served them. If there are any minimum essentials, they are the facts that no one could miss if he explored the field of human knowledge to any degree at all. It is not so much that these items are essential as that they are unavoidable.

To illustrate this point, a teacher of history asked me if I would be willing that the learner should know nothing about Abraham Lincoln. Certainly a knowledge and appreciation of Lincoln would add to the richness of the living of most people. But I do not believe that anyone could explore American History ever so slightly without encountering Lincoln. And I also believe that if he could do so he would be able to live happily and successfully without knowledge of Lincoln. The person who asked the question was stretching the point to absurdity by the choice of his example. There are many more obscure facts of American History that are often treated as essential. I sometimes ask my students how many know who Israel Putnam was. Almost never does anyone know. Yet when I studied American History, knowledge of Putnam was an essential, and if I had not known who he was I would not have gotten "credit." There is nothing wrong with knowing who Putnam was. In fact, I think knowing about him has added to the richness of life, and to my feeling for the men and women of the American Revolution. I imagine his wife must have had eventually to unhitch the team which he left attached to the plow when he went to fight the Redcoats. But I encounter people by the hundreds who are getting along quite as well as I, and are quite ignorant of the fact that any such person ever lived.

Subject matter is the medium through which the adult mind of the teacher and the immature mind of the learner find communion. It is the vehicle for growth. Knowledge is not power in itself, but knowledge which enables the individual to function more effectively adds to his power. The particulars of subject matter must be those for which the learner can find functional use in his own concrete world.

CHAPTER VIII

How Shall We Live Together?

As each of us is unique, both in purpose and in experiential background, and as we really can have no precisely common world with any of our fellows, what kind of life can we lead that will be tenable? What shall our relationship to our fellows be? What arrangement of society will best enable each to be unique, as he must be, and yet enter into a workable relationship with others? What does our modern knowledge of perception and knowing demand of us?

Some people react to these questions by saying that if these concepts concerning the nature of perception are true, then the Nazi philosophy is indicated and justified. They say that if everyone has his own purpose and his own world, then someone will have to take over and run things in order that we may have an orderly society.

There are really only two ways by which the individual may be controlled. Either he must be controlled by someone else, or he must govern himself. He may govern himself by seeking only his own immediate good, without regard for others, or even to their conscious and deliberate detriment. Or he may govern himself through common agreement with others, and in the light of his own and their needs and purposes.

Those who think that dictatorship is indicated by the

demonstrated uniqueness of the individual overlook the fact that individual purpose is basic to perception. The demonstrations in perception have shown that purpose is at the base of the selective process by which we perceive. When a dictator takes over, he furnishes the purpose. This is precisely why dictatorships are unsuccessful in the long run. They violate the basis for knowing. The human organism is always trying to circumvent the dictator so that the process of functioning individual purpose can go on.

How then can one learn to follow orders, as he has to in many of the world's employment situations? Does he not, in the working world, have to get his orders from above, and follow them simply because they are orders?

There seems to be ample evidence that the autocratic nature of our society is unsatisfactory to the people concerned, both those giving the orders and those receiving them.[1] Our whole situation of industrial unrest seems to point to this fact. This indicates that we will be more successful if we examine and modify our institutions than we will be if we attempt to modify man's basic way of knowing.

There are many industrial plants and business organizations in operation where the employees and employers are partners, where both have a part in planning, and where both enjoy a share in the success of their enterprise. These organizations are almost always without labor strife. Far more common is the working situation where there is no sharing either in what is to be done or in the goods that come from success. Millions work in these situations, but they do not give their best to the enterprise. They may fight or strike. Most often, how-

[1] Those dubious on this point should read "The Social Problems of an Industrial Civilization," by Elton Mayo, Harvard Press, 1945.

ever, they retire into themselves. Their jobs become motions they go through in order to secure the means of livelihood. Their real living takes place after the day's work is over. The job is devoid of fulfillment.

Nor does the one who sets the purposes for others seem to fare much better. The boss, it would seem, should be happy whether anyone else is or not. But there is much evidence that the process is not good for him either. He lives in fear that the dammed-up purposes of those under him will break loose. This makes him inordinately suspicious of his fellow men, whom he needs to trust. This fear and suspicion lead to acts which drive him away from his workers. Aggravated suspicion is a mental disease, and he often becomes paranoid. What seems on the surface to have been a successful career results in great unhappiness. Sometimes his body refuses to contend any longer with an unsupportable mind, and he dies of high blood pressure, stomach ulcers, or a heart attack.

The Nazi, or autocratic way of life is untenable because it rejects the fact of individual unique purpose. If it were possible, a situation approaching anarchy would be more in keeping with what we know about the nature of the human organism and how it functions. Each organism would then follow its own way without regard to any other.[2]

The fruit of each individual doing exactly as he pleases with his own good always in mind would be intense competition. He would be bent on getting ahead of the other fellow. But if competition is inherent in the situation, so are lying, stealing, and many other antisocial activities.

---

[2] In fairness to the old Anarchist political party, this is not what they advocated. They wanted each of us to live on such a high plane that government would be unnecessary. This would require acute cognizance of the importance and the rights of other people.

If one is concerned only with his own immediate welfare, there is no reason why he should not lie and steal to the degree that he can make it work. We try from the cradle to inhibit lying and stealing, but we encourage equally natural and equally unsocial competition. In this regard, though not in others, we cling to the law of the jungle.

This does not mean that competitive games are bad for people. The question arises as to whether it is really a game, or whether it is "for keeps." Each of us demands his place in the sun, and it may be good therapy to exhaust one's competitive urges in games. But the competition of life is not a game; it is deadly serious, and it has the damage of another at its base. Even games can so result. Perhaps that is what has happened in college football. Originally it was played for fun, but then the commercial aspects of the game arose, and now it is too often played for keeps. For this reason, many of the boys who play it do not like it, although they did enjoy it when they played with others informally on the playground.

The anarchistic theory might hold up were it not for the fact that we live in a social world. We do not know that man is naturally a social being, but we do know that whether he likes it or not (and he appears to like it), he is born into a social situation. In the social situation he cannot successfully go forward alone. He must learn that the social good is the greatest good for him as an individual, and that he can best achieve his place in the sun with the help of others and by helping others. This calls for cooperation as a basic way of life.[3] With the cooperation of man's fellows, he can live in keeping with his unique

[3] For a succinct discussion of the values involved in cooperation, see a statement by Howard A. Lane in "Group Planning in Education," Department of Supervision and Curriculum, National Education Association, 1945, Chapter I.

purposes and experiential background. He can seek his own good through the achievement of the good of the whole. He can lend himself and spend himself in the accomplishment of what is necessary for him in relationship to what is possible and necessary for those with whom he is associated.

Since we have no common world, we can only cooperate with others as we can get communion with them. Communion is the appreciation, so far as possible, of the position, point of view, and attitude of others. It is essential to any sharing of purpose. In order to assist us in achieving communion with others and coming as close as possible to a common world with them, we have various means of communication. Speech is the most universal of these, but by no means the only one. Language and speech are so essential to communion that we have great difficulty in achieving any degree of commonalty with those who do not speak our language. Since this is true, and since we must inhabit the same globe with them, we need to try all the harder to use as many other avenues of communication as possible when we deal with those of other languages and customs.

The necessity of taking the social situation into account has been greatly increased in the last century. A hundred years ago people did not live so closely together, and anyone who found other people too insufferable could go off into the wilderness by himself. But the industrial age demands that we live together. In this age we have become highly specialized, and as we have specialized we have become interdependent. The frontiersman was not specialized, and did everything for himself; not very well, to be sure, but after a fashion. But now we cannot do everything for ourselves. The more unlike us another is, the more we need him. I, being a teacher, am not so dependent on other teachers as I am on the watchmaker or the shoe-maker. I can do a better job teaching my child than I can making her shoes. Then it follows that I should value those who are different from me, rather than valuing most those who are like me.

The plea for cooperation as a basic way of life is called for by the nature of the human organism thrust into a highly social and complex world. It is not a softhearted cry for Utopia, an other-worldly Sunday school lesson. It is a hardheaded suggestion for a way of life by which we may survive. It is as factual as a choice between green fields and rubble.

It is the only way of life which we have never tried on a large scale, and becomes our only remaining alternative. We have tried the competition of the jungle, and numerous forms of authoritarianism. The cooperative way is not the easy way, else we surely would have tried it. It is the hard way because it calls for sensitivity to what lies outside our own organisms. The peace which is implied in the cooperative way of life is not easy. It has always been easier for us to go to war than to maintain peace. Very often in the past, when our problems of getting along with others have become difficult, we have taken the easy way, and gone to war.

ARE THERE TOO MANY OF US?

Perhaps the world has grown too large for us, and the human mind is incapable of coping with the problems of such a world inhabited by so many people. We often say that, with increased communication and rapid travel, the world has grown small. This is true in the sense that we can now go from New York to Shanghai in less time than it took to go from New York to Boston in colonial times, and that a rocket bomb makes greater speed than did the

Crusaders. But in another sense, whenever we increase communication, we enlarge the number of people an individual has to deal with, and so the world grows larger. Now the individual is forced to cope with all of the other people in the world, and his world is enormous.

This is forcefully illustrated even in the lives of many now living. When I was a boy on the farm I knew scarcely anyone who lived more than three miles away. The people were all much alike—of the same race, religion, and occupation. I therefore had to accommodate myself to very few others, and mostly people much like myself. Now I not only know and have to deal with literally thousands, but I have to take into account every other human being on the earth. I cannot now afford to be unaware of or unconcerned about anyone anywhere. If we bring our former limited selves to these larger responsibilities, failure confronts us.

If there were only a few of us, and we were cast away together on a desert isle, we would quickly see that our best interest lay in the interest of the whole group. We would discern at once that we must cooperate or die. Food and water would be scarce, so we would divide the supply on the basis of need, not according to who had the most money or any preferred position. We would come to value each person of the group for the unique contribution to the common good that he is able to make. We would not ask about his color, religion, or ancestry. Seeking personal gain at the cost of one's fellows would become the cardinal sin. We would, of course, hope and expect to be rescued.

We *are* a group cast away on an island in space. This island is going we know not where. We do know that it is to be our abode for good or ill for all of life as we know it. We know we shall not be rescued. Simple logic would indicate that our best salvation lies in working together for the interest of all, and that each one of us is a priceless asset to the success of the whole.

We are more fortunate than those cast upon the desert isle. For this spherical island, hurtling through space, is not a desert, but indescribably rich. It is warmed by a sun which gives out tremendous supplies of energy, and is placed at just the right distance away so that we get enough and not too much energy. It is the *good* earth. It abounds with all of the good things that human life can use, in such prodigal quantities that there is more than enough for all. The waters of its land are sweet, and its air is wholesome and lifegiving. The goods of earth are further arranged in nature so that wherever we look we see beauty. Often earth, sea, sky, and sun combine their efforts to lift man's soul with a glory that beggars words.

It would appear that on such an island, such a vast rich world, we should all be completely happy. The common good of us all would impel us to see to it that none of us needed for anything. But instead we see most of our people ill-provided for from our vast store. Hunger, nakedness, homelessness, and disease are commonplace. Medicines which would heal the suffering of millions are withheld. All of the scourges that result from want, both in body and in spirit, are rampant. Instead of concentrating on getting the good things of life to all of us, we give our attention to strife over small bits of them. Instead of making, through cooperation, two blades of grass grow where one grew before, we fall to quarreling over the one, until, seared by our venom, it withers and dies.

For some reason we seem to have lost sight of the fact that the most important part of our world is the people in it. The common people are our great common denominator. We get nowhere when we complain about

the people, as many of us, especially teachers, are so prone
to do. Since people are the most important factors in the
world, and since human progress is the net result of the
efforts of the whole human race, a human being must be
an asset. If he is an asset, we must act toward him as though
he had value. We do not now, in many instances, act as
though all human beings have value. That is why we feel
the need for setting up all sorts of exclusions, restrictions,
and discriminations. When we hear that another human
being is headed for our shores, or for our precious little
community where nobody lives except those who are
just like us, we react with fear and erect barriers. We do
not feel happy to know that another person, with his
unique contribution, has come to live and work among
us, and thus enrich us.

It is perhaps true that some individuals have met so
much adversity in life that they are damaged and are not
now functioning as assets. But they have the potentialities
of human beings, and these are great, as evidenced by the
sum of human accomplishment. These less fortunate fellow men, instead of being cast out, must be seen as potential assets, and their feet placed upon the paths of
growth and achievement—placed there as we would
handle something of great value.

PEOPLE ARE IMPORTANT

If people are the most important asset on our island
whirling in space, then human relations become our most
important study. The significant fact about any citizen
then becomes his attitude toward other people. Does a
man think his neighbor one to be feared, watched, and, if
need be, crushed? Or does he look upon his neighbor as
possessing most of the virtues which he attributes to him-

self? Does he regard his neighbor as one whom he may help, and by whom he may be helped?

We hear a great deal in our present society about the importance of human relations. Cooperation is implied in human relations, because authoritarianism does not take the needs, will, or purpose of the individual into account. But too often we mean how to get along with others so we can get the most out of them. How can I know my fellow man better, so that I can better compete with him, more surely beat him at his own game? This is merely an insidious form of exploitation. Until we can come to seek better rapport and communion with our fellows for the good of both, and to our mutual growth and advantage, we have not taken the first step in real human relations. Indeed, we are headed in the wrong direction.

This evil concept of human relations (how can I know my fellow man better so that I can best exploit him) turns our attention away from ourselves and onto others. It leads us to look for the reasons for our ills in others, not in ourselves. We are of course all right, and we must understand the quirks of others, so as to cope with them to our advantage. The fact of the matter is that the essence of the trouble lies in each of us, and further, that these ills in us might be the easier ones for us to modify. We might then be more moderate in projecting blame on Russian, employer, laborer, child, neighbor, Negro, white, and start our reconstruction where it is most feasible—with ourselves.

How then shall we live together? How can we be unique, and also meet the demands of a social world, where the uniqueness of others must be taken into account? Surely not by surrendering our purposes to that of another, and even surrendering our choice of experience. Surely not by trying to "go it alone," without regard for the good we can derive from others, as well as the help we may be to them. Surely not by the asocial law of the jungle, the primitive and uncivilized survival of the fittest.

Civilization must mean more than gadgets, more than tiled bathrooms and atomic bombs. It must imply attainment of ethics higher than those held by the uncivilized. It must mean the finding of the greatest personal good by the achievement of the greatest good for all. For education, it must mean a new set of patterns, built from the cooperative, rather than the punitive and competitive, point of view. It must mean the accomplishment of purpose through cognizance of and adjustment to the purposes of others. Only in seeking these goods can we become civilized.

Index